[6-]
12
35904
R

An Invitation to Our Times

BOOKS BY MITCHELL S. ROSS

THE LITERARY POLITICIANS

AN INVITATION TO OUR TIMES

An Invitation to Our Times

MITCHELL S. ROSS

DOUBLEDAY & COMPANY, INC.
GARDEN CITY, NEW YORK

1980

For my brother, Andy,
in honor of a thousand and one nights of argument

ISBN: 0-385-15031-8
Library of Congress Catalog Card Number 79–7609
Copyright © 1980 by Mitchell Scott Ross
All Rights Reserved
Printed in the United States of America
First Edition

Contents

An Invitation to Our Times

Greeting

I welcome you to the 1980s. Those who have recently come of age know nothing of Richard Nixon the national disgrace, but are instead aware of Nixon the Oxford debater, or Nixon the saint of Hyden, Kentucky, or even Nixon the polite guest at White House functions. Children have learned to walk and speak while believing that the American presidency is an office naturally occupied by the likes of Gerald Ford and Jimmy Carter. The Vietnam war has finally ceased to seem either a heroic crusade on behalf of the Free World, or a monstrous violation of the nation's moral fiber. I am sure that some of my fellow citizens merely think of it as something which threatens to break out between the Russians and the Chinese. The notion that these countries are partners in a worldwide Communist conspiracy is no longer even good for a joke.

Slightly older Americans now have their Vietnam war packaged for them in such a movie as *The Deer Hunter,* in which the director does not make the slightest effort to co-ordinate the movements of his characters with known historical fact. The whole affair comes off as little more than a bad and bloody dream, which is about the way the American public has come to regard it. I expect that soon the figures of Abbie Hoffman, Dean Rusk and General Westmoreland will sit in comfortable, jolly poses in some wax museum, each in his own way calling up memories of a lively and colorful era and serving the national passion for nostalgia which substitutes for historical sense.

The air is clearing. Black folks are talking about becoming first-rate Americans by making fortunes for themselves. The feminist upheaval is being rapidly reduced to the level of a televised sherry commercial, in which She invites Steve over for a drink, and looks thoroughly smug about the whole thing. The late radical Jane Fonda has been reborn as Jane Fonda the Hollywood star, who strips down to a bikini without bothering to assert that she is making a public statement by doing so.

Anyone who has managed to beat inflation by practicing an interesting profession is also presumed to have a notable soul. For example, the sports heroes of the land grow richer and more righteous. Bill Walton, perhaps the last living representative of the counterculture (no one else can so completely afford the luxury), flies off to the Philippines to prophesy the extinction of the monkey-eating eagle. Other athletes have adopted similar poses, and imagine themselves leading their countrymen back to God. Reggie Jackson, designated superstar, with no better lifetime statistics than those of Ted Kluszewski and Roy Sievers, expresses public confidence that the Almighty will protect him from perfidy and Billy Martin. The stars of the Los Angeles Dodgers slug it out in their clubhouse, and afterward one of them apologizes publicly and thanks God for the existence of the other one.

Other symptoms of the Republic's spiritual temper are hard to sort out. Revelations of murderous cults and fleeings into the jungle have upset people's notion that whatever makes you feel good is probably good for you. The Catholics have got themselves a Pope who has composed phenomenological texts and battled Communists but yet seems impressed with the style of American politicians to the point of emulation. The Jews, it appears, will have to refine their analogies of Germany and Araby . . . but I am rushing ahead, and I want to look backward—at least far enough backward so that we can arrive at some general understanding and sit down comfortably at the same table.

1

The Mystique
of Freedom

Show me the man who will state "the national condition," and I will show you a fool. As I survey the landscape from my carefully manicured estates, I see much incomprehensible movement. The populace runs about in a perpetual state of alarm. Two steps forward are followed by three looks backward. A bold uncertainty marks the age, but who will argue beyond that?

A thousand commentators try. There are all those grim faces reporting and analyzing the news on television, intimating their own sagacity with every utterance. There are the legions of the professoriat, gathering their thoughts in solemn journals, attempting to assay the current quality of this "new man, . . . an American," as Crèvecoeur called him long ago. There are Presidents and would-be Presidents of the United States diagnosing severe ailments and prescribing cure-alls which they feel uniquely equipped to administer. But what do they really know?

In my capacity as a sage, I have occasionally worked up the eloquence to talk of freedom, its meaning and purpose, and I confess that on such occasions I have never felt lighter in my head nor more dazzling on my feet. But such displays always leave me with a dreadful hangover. I wonder where I have been and what I have said. I worry that I shall end up like Aleksandr Solzhenitsyn, denouncing my sanctuary and missing the point. I do suspect, however, that we Americans endow our lives with a powerful notion which I label the mystique of freedom. This is essentially the belief, spread impartially among spartans and hedonists within the Republic, that Americans understand freedom best because they know the most about it. Americans appear to believe that they have invented freedom, and that its appearance elsewhere in the world should be regarded as imperfect imitation. As a man of detachment with pretensions to civility, I try harder than most people to divorce my thoughts from this mystique. As a patriot, however, I frequently surrender to it. With my ambition to be known as a man of the world, I gladly suffer the slings of foreigners arguing for the greatness of their lands. I admit freely to the superior charm of the French, the supreme beauty of the Italians, and the overwhelming strength and soulfulness of the Slavs. But I do not willingly permit myself to be lectured on the subject of freedom by any son of Cameroon or Greece, and I will hear an Englishman on the subject only if he permits me to grunt at the conclusion of his speech.

In the Parnassian regions inhabited by intellectuals, some of the liveliest battles have been fought over the question of what is behind the life of these States. The air is filled with great explanations, which are regarded by the populace with warmth and even enthusiasm. Consider the recent cases of Charles Reich, Doctor of Laws at Yale University and the author of a treatise called *The Greening of America,* and Alvin Toffler, a professional journalist of severe and handsome gaze whose gift to the nation was a tome called *Future Shock.* These gentlemen have been greatly celebrated and enriched by literate Americans. It is instructive to note how they achieved their enviable fates.

The Greening of America represented the blowsiest sort of abstract thinking. Here was a text presumably devoted to social analysis which was devoid of particular references as it could possibly be. Here was an unseemly regurgitation of a thousand doctoral theses, some of them by economists, others by political scientists, and the rest written by sociologists and future professors of English. Here was thinking aerated and finally preserved in the form of Consciousness I, II and III. There was much blabbing about the revolution of our times, and the New Man being formed in Consciousness III. Such talk suggests to people that their own lives are not really messy but heroic, and part of a vast social upheaval. Everyone else, meanwhile, is presumably leading a life of quiet desperation, and so the struggle must be carried on. Professor Reich went about his business with the solemnity of a Marine Corps Band director conducting fanfares at a presidential inauguration. For this his readers seemed grateful. The important thing was the way in which he reupholstered their self-esteem.

Toffler was similarly dour in *Future Shock.* Amid that breathless hymn to the whirlkönig, a few sound chords were struck. His thesis—that America and the world were changing so fast that we could hardly be expected to keep up with ourselves—had a certain plausibility and a limited usefulness. But Toffler did not know when to leave well enough alone, and in the end he was overcome by a fever of sententiousness. One recognized that what was at work was less a social analyst than an efficient computer, programmed to process materials demonstrating the rapidity of change and to ignore everything else.

In each case, an ecclesiastical tone made it clear that the morality of the Republic was the fundamental issue. Professor Reich regarded the sinners as those trapped within the mentality of the corporate state: these were the holdouts inside Consciousness II. The saints were the free spirits who were not so much interested in self-reliance (these were the neanderthals of Consciousness I) as they were anxious to burst free from corporate bondage into an atmosphere of common trust and shared concerns. All this was given a fine dialectical burnishing: no need to identify saints and sinners as such, and risk disorienting the public. Toffler, in his turn, left no doubt that those who were plugged into change deserved a kinder fate than those who resisted it. The first and most important step toward righteousness was the total acceptance of Alvin Toffler's thesis. Whether you did or not depended on whether you were a man of the future or a man of the past—but there was no question that the march to heaven was forward.

It should be remembered that the sermon is the oldest American literary form. Its appeal has been consistent. If he could have learned to modulate his voice before the television cameras, Cotton Mather might have enjoyed a distinguished career in the America of the late twentieth century. The mystique of freedom descends directly from those visionaries who failed to blink when the image of the City on the Hill danced before their eyes. It embraces a dream of moral perfection. Of course, with few exceptions, the American is the least philosophical of men, and when he thinks grandly, he invariably thinks badly. But the quest has left its public marks, from the Declaration of Independence to the Gettysburg Address, from the Fourteen Points of Woodrow Wilson to the ruminations of the deacon Carter. There have been the wars fought in freedom's name, many of them shabby and disappointing but all of them provoking wonderful musings on the nature and purpose of the American Republic. The literati have similarly indulged themselves, from Emerson's exhortation for "the American scholar" to the passage on the "whole crisis of Christianity in America" which concludes the mountebank Mailer's *The Armies of the Night*.

The lifetime of these States has not been long. The grandparents of our grandparents were perking when Andrew Jackson was President of the United States, and, if longevity runs in the family, when Thomas Jefferson and John Adams were still alive. And so these efforts to absorb the meaning and divine the destiny of America resemble the attempts of puberty-laden youths to master the lyrics of their favorite songs. Each of us has an ancestor who hopped aboard some boat without any idea of his future, and we are still trying to crawl out of the confusion. In the meantime it is important for Americans to believe that they are living in a great country, and that the fate of mankind depends upon their ability to resolve all moral dilemmas in a satisfactory manner.

Combined with the physical vastness of the nation, the mystique of freedom has inclined Americans to experiment with various modes of life. The economics of capitalism, with their emphasis on constant change, have also contributed to America's amusing instability. The prosperity of the last several decades has encouraged the citizenry to lance its Old World boils and powder the bluenoses of its puritanical past. Legal sanction has been granted to almost every fashion of behavior, and social sanction has usually followed. Sometimes the sanction is confined to a single region, but in any case there is room for everyone who can pay his way. The Mormons would find the going rough in the North End of Boston, but they have settled comfortably into control of the state of Utah. An astrologer who cannot pay her bills in Grand Rapids can simply hightail it into Chicago. A pair of sadomasochists, weary of stealing visits to each other's farmhouse in the great state of Kansas, can safely bash each other around a converted warehouse near the Greenwich Village docks.

In this sense everyone has been liberated. Was there ever a time in human history when it was harder for one person to tell another how to live his life? Who will dare to enforce such views? An American today need only gather together a group which shares his predilections, and he will find himself not merely tolerated but encouraged. We are as much at ease as we choose to be. Telephones, televisions, airplanes and superhighways permit us to make connections with events elsewhere as rapidly as we want to make them. Only the poor folks miss out on the fun, and in this country it is sometimes hard to determine who is really poor, and what is the precise nature of his handicap.

Of course it is not all that simple. Americans would be less anxious to find out the meaning of things if they were more sure of themselves. But I consider myself free because I am required to do nothing except pay my bills and my taxes. I say required, because there are allurements on all sides. A thousand committed men and women compete for my attention. But no law deprives me of volition, and no overpowering moral code commands me to move in one direction rather than another. I may choose my snares, and, when I do so, I can count on someone being present to embrace me and assure me of my righteousness. This is how we have enlivened our era, and henceforth I will concern myself with the ironies and ambiguities of the situation. This will amount to something less than a State of the Union message, but, if it makes you feel better, you may go ahead and sound some ruffles and flourishes.

2

The National Landscape

I. SON OF MICHIGAN

I am a citizen of the state of Michigan, born in Detroit, raised there and in its environs, and trained to regard the world from its geographical perspective. I have barnstormed the Republic, touched down in almost every citadel of European Christendom, and crept through lands controlled by Mohammedans. A thousand impressions have been etched upon my mind, and a hundred challenges to my cherished assumptions have been endured. These have been but alterations of the original images formed in childhood and youth. In any case it is difficult to sort out general attitudes from those peculiar to one's region, and the invasion of television makes the job impossible.

But my first impressions of the social world were formed in that raucous metropolis which regards the automobile as fervently as the ancient Israelites ever regarded the golden calf. Jehovah's opinion not having been consulted, the consequences of this idolatry remain unclear. A Detroiter's horizons form over the waters of the Great Lakes. It is strange that the city of Detroit and the state of Michigan are so readily identified as part of the great, fertile and unexciting stretch of territory called the Midwest. A recent President of the United States from Grand Rapids helped to reinforce this image of dull decency, but the natural character of Michigan is much spicier than that of other Midwestern states. The lower half of the Lower Peninsula is, to be sure, an uninteresting if productive expanse, but cruising northward one's attention is quickly arrested by the graceful, arching hills, and by the first sign of the heroic pine trees. Further north the eye is ravished by the sight of these pines, now set on grander hills than before and approached all around by lakes of every size and description. Even further north is the wilderness of the Upper Peninsula, still prowled by bears, lumberjacks, and other rude animals, as in the old days. In the northern regions, and all along the lakeshores, there are hints of the wild and strange in the life of the state.

The social life of Michigan also makes it an anomaly. There are undeniably a fair number of boresome rural characters, inclined to answer questions with a "Yup" or a "Nope." There are certainly a fair number of citizens who are struck dumb by such names as Johann Sebastian Bach, Michelangelo Buonarroti, and even Woodrow Wilson. But the quality of these characters is still a shade higher than that of comparable ignoramuses in the South, the Rocky Mountain states, or on the Eastern Shore of Maryland. Michigan could not be judged dull or backward by any sensible standard. The city of Detroit is in this sense representative of the state as a whole. It is without doubt among the ugliest of American cities, a place where buildings have been erected and razed with no more regard to public decency than is felt by the tanners of Fez who foul the air with their labors. It is a city largely filled with tedious housing, some of it downright insulting to eyes which have examined the meanest of Parisian arrondissements. Its initial charms are few, and its efforts to allure a newcomer are like those of an old vaudeville queen with varicose veins. And yet it is without question one of the most intriguing cities in the land, perhaps in the entire world, a place to which I cannot return after an absence without a sense of wonder and puzzlement. In addition to the curious events that enliven city life everywhere, Detroit is a town of merchants who believe themselves princes; of black Caesars born, it sometimes seems, overnight; of athletes exalted to heights which would have amazed Wagner's Siegfried, the hero of heroes. But it is above all a city in which plain folks earn a better living than anywhere else in the land, and where the consequences are played out daily. Observing the flow of the city's life, a man of means and fastidiously cultivated leisure could not possibly imagine that the place was designed for him, but he can sit back and enjoy the show all the same.

Chicago, Detroit's gaudier rival to the west, can claim many of the same characteristics for itself. But the time is long past when the student of cities could examine Chicago with the same cold eye that he can cast upon Detroit. The place is too vast, too hard to handle. It is in a sense even more enormous than New York, considering the latter's division into five distinctive boroughs. Then, too, Chicago's economy is too varied to permit the same isolation of industrial qualities that Detroit encourages. The relative wickedness of the two towns I do not presume to judge; that they stand apart from the other cities of the midlands is apparent. They cannot be compared with Cleveland, Buffalo, Pittsburgh or St. Louis. A certain dynamism sets them apart. Their affairs are crucial to the affairs of the nation at large. Their ambitions, presumptions, failures and achievements must be duly noted by any man who desires to detect the nation's drift.

In recent years Detroit has found itself singled out for special attention by the national press. It is an honor most Detroiters would have happily renounced, as the purpose of the press was to create a symbol of the Decline of the American City. More recently the mood of the publicists has changed, and the American City is now seen to be resurrecting itself. Detroit has claimed some attention by hoisting a set of towers and calling it a Renaissance Center, but the first law of journalism is that misery makes better news than happiness. A few pleasant notices have not balanced the scales; the impression of Detroit throughout the nation remains for the most part unpleasant.

The citizen of the region, if he is not demoralized by this civic abuse, naturally regards it with bemusement. It is not so much that the prophecies of decline and resurrection seem grotesquely in error as that all the rhetorical thrashing about bears such slight relation to the life he sees all around him. Perhaps it is the same with cities and communities of all types in the Republic; I cannot say. But certainly it is so with all cities of great ambition—those places which desire to be recognized as more than mere blobs on a map, and prefer to be known as incubators of civilization. A citizen of New York, Boston, Washington, Chicago, Los Angeles, San Francisco, Houston, Atlanta or Detroit does not wish to feel that he is spending his days in a location without significance to the world. Through his city (or, in current context, his metropolitan region) he seeks some justification of his own life, some sense of the glory and

pain of human existence, some connection between the in-
congruities of his waking hours. And so he may reflect on
his civic condition, and wonder if his world is collapsing or
rebounding; he may consider whether or not great dramas
are being played out in the surrounding streets—even if, in
the end, he can do no more than nod his head and resume
his business.

The Detroiter, as I say, is as accustomed to such
reflections as any American, and by now the various public
pronouncements on his civic condition have no more than a
hollow resonance. Only a New Yorker, who enters each
day convinced that he is dissolving his hours in the most
terrible and magnificent of environments, pays less attention to these conventional boosters and deflations. The
effect of this is simple: the Detroiter has been unwittingly
prepared to face the world with an attitude of austere realism. If he corrupts his thoughts with ideologies and the dis-
guised metaphysics of sociologists, he deserves a sounder
whipping than a member of any other species of genus
Americanus. The facts of life in a great industrial republic
are laid out plainly before him: the facts of gigantic corpo-
rations and magnificent, swaggering labor unions; of the
black man on the rise and the white man balancing his
toleration with his resentment; of the passion for sport and
the grudging acceptance of the arts; of the distrust of city
life which is itself built into the making of American cities.
He has heard the most distinguished commentators in the
land inform him of his condition, and he has concluded
that they are muddleheaded. Whether inside the city proper
or in one of its suburbs, he senses that he is in the midst
of enduring the characteristic American experience.

Thus I account for a fair portion of my own presumption regarding the affairs of the nation: my native city has
served as a hothouse for realistic minds. And, as I say, it is

set inside a state which has been given its midwestern designation a bit too carelessly. The Great Lakes isolate Michigan, making it stranger and even dreamier territory than is generally supposed.

II.   CITY, SUBURB, COUNTRY

It has often been remarked that a curious quality of the American is his restlessness, his inclination to move freely and resettle himself in strange locales without giving the matter more than a moment's thought. Forgetting for a moment its hordes of Eastern Europeans, southern Balkanites and Arabs, the city of Detroit includes numerous immigrants from Appalachia and points south, and its suburbs are filled with successful laborers and executives from every corner of the land. It has been inferred from such developments that the American cares less for his physical surroundings than other breeds of men; commentators of dark temperament have gone so far as to argue that such rootlessness portends the ultimate dissolution of the Republic into small civil wars between strangers. In any case American mobility is but another manifestation of the mystique of freedom, this time embodied in the notion that one's place of residence will make one freer and better equipped to pursue happiness.

Historically there was evidence to support such a notion. A black man raised in rural Mississippi in the early 1900s, for example, might have reasonably supposed that his life would be better in a northern city: he might find a job which paid a decent wage, and he would avoid ending his life by being lynched. A girl in Bismarck, North Dakota, who acquired a taste for grand opera would quickly realize that her life was meant to be lived elsewhere. But today the southern black man might manage to become mayor of his home town, and the girl in Bismarck might satisfy her passion for *Aïda* with stereophonic records and viewings of public television. While these States have by no means achieved perfect homogeneity, the differences within them have been substantially narrowed.

Even so the American remains the quintessential man on the move, now riding in compact cars instead of wagon trains, but still dreaming of the great future ahead of him in some new place. In contrast, the American farmer who lifts a handful of dirt from his land and thrusts it toward the sky with a prayer to God upon his lips is thought to be very odd indeed. Such is the national character, as we have grown to understand it.

But if he is inclined to move about, the American has by no means renounced the privilege to identify himself according to his place of residence. As I say, he wants to feel that his city is viewed with interest by the rest of the world; it is an extension of his private desire to feel loved. Where the American seems to fail is in his aesthetic sense; the desire to make his city lovely and notable is unaccompanied by practical knowledge of how to make it happen. Consequently, even the most physically charming among large American cities—Boston, San Francisco and Washington—are second-rate in comparison with the cities of Europe. It is not merely a question of age, as some would have it. The great towns of Germany are for practical purposes newer than American cities, having been shattered by our bombs during the late war against Hitler. Despite the miserable stucco exteriors of many of their buildings, Cologne, Frankfurt, Munich, Hamburg and Berlin are far livelier entities than American towns of comparable size. Even the vaunted excitement of New York—the rush of people on its streets, the noise of traffic, the thrill of active humanity thrown together in a small space—is exposed after dark as an absurdity. At nine o'clock of an evening, there are as many people on a side street in one of Paris's fashionable arrondissements as on the whole of Fifth Avenue in the Fifties.

The reason for this, I suspect, is that the American's desire to exalt his town ranks low on his list of priorities. He has, for example, traditionally been more interested in isolating himself in a private home than in sharing space in an apartment building. The idea that a row of town houses constitutes the best solution to the problem of limited space has never really taken hold here. It had a run in the nineteenth century, and the brownstone style left a permanent mark on New York City, but this was little more than the architectural equivalent of New England Swedenborgianism: a slight variation of the European mode. Once the nation started to spread out, the style of urban domestic architecture involved a detached house surrounded by a garden and lawn—in brief, a suburban style. Consider examples from early in the twentieth century: Detroit's Boston-Edison district, Chicago's Hyde Park, Los Angeles' Hancock Park: all are indistinguishable from more recent suburban developments in their general design; their age alone makes them representative of the past.

The suburban style reflected the American's desire to set himself apart and assert his individuality in the character of his home. The "suburban revolution" which began in the 1950s was like most other American revolutions: a slight acceleration of a process begun long before. The only really notable development came later, when companies began building offices in the suburbs, so that today it is characteristic for an American to live in one suburb, work in another, and often ignore the doings inside the old city altogether. He flees higher taxes and the greater threat of crime, and he does not think twice about it.

In contrast, the European attitude toward cities is more deferential. The texture of city life there represents the quality of life in general. The European does not suppose that the methods of suburbia can be imposed on the city proper. He preserves old structures in a zealous manner which all right-thinking Americans thought eccentric until only a few years ago. Even today, it is difficult to locate a city father susceptible to the idea that a building deserves to stand because it is lovelier than whatever will replace it, and can be made just as useful.

But it is nonsense to suppose that, because the American resides in a suburban style, he is naturally a suburbanite. Such might be said of Englishmen, a tidier and more cautious breed than ourselves. The American suburbanite merely represents a compromise with his instincts. He believes that he hears the call of the wild. He thinks of himself as the natural man, called away from his true home by grim economic necessities, and eager to return to nature at the first opportunity. This is the main reason why American cities are so inferior to the cities of Europe: their residents do not see them as natural habitats, and so regard them as carelessly as they regard other things they do not really care about. I do not argue that the American is inherently a rube or a slob. He may in fact fuss greatly over his own home, lawn and garden. But his attitude will be that the city would function well and attain beauty if only his neighbors did the same thing. He scorns civic planning as redolent of socialism, and so the city planner is invariably a third-rate jobber, devoid of a sense of beauty. Upon being told that London, Paris and Vienna were not built by socialists, the American responds righteously that things are done differently here in these great States, that here the individual is king. Tacitly he acknowledges that the mystique of freedom has overpowered his thoughts and robbed him of his common sense. Consequently it is no accident that whenever an American city achieves some distinctive appearance, some urban boss will most likely have got control of the town and made a sham of its democratic pretensions. Consider the case of Chicago—particularly its lakefront—and Mayor Richard J. Daley. In the past quartercentury, no man made greater sport of the democratic pieties, and none did more to make his city handsome.

As the political machines vanish, the odds on improving the appeal of American cities will grow longer. The natural sleaziness of American civic democracy will be exacerbated by ignorant federal interventions, and the civilized American will find himself looking outside of cities for his pleasures. This development distresses me, as I am a city man by temperament. I contemplate three hours in the companionship of a fishing pole with horror. I flee from the foul odors of the barnyard. I yearn for a *Nozze di Figaro*, followed by strawberries and cream, and champagne and a cigar, and a stroll along grand boulevards, before falling happily into bed with my white tie drooping rakishly from my collar. By every indication, if I am to have my *Nozze* at all in the American city of the future, I will be lucky to refresh my palate with Milk Duds and concentrated orange juice before scrambling through the night to recover my car before its tires are spirited away by youths indifferent to Mozart and dead set against da Ponte. I will have to drive past hideous housing developments before arriving home. I will have to struggle to resurrect my image of Cherubino, and to recall the lament of "Dove sono" before nervously attempting to sleep.

More likely I will remain in wooded seclusion with my

stereophonic equipment—not because I too feel the call of nature, but because I begin to feel pushed toward it. In the past few decades the American resistance to city life has resulted in the palpable degeneration of urban existence. All the recent blabbering about urban homesteading and the return of bright young people to the cities offers little more than faint promise. Increasingly the most pleasant environments in the United States are quite apart from the cities. At this moment, for example, I am inside a condominium apartment on the west coast of Florida. I can watch the waters of the Gulf of Mexico roll toward a beach on which my feet can land in three minutes. I can be prancing on a tennis court in even less time. The apartment is situated on an island which has been incorporated into a town; the cities of Sarasota and Bradenton are nearby, but separate. The island itself provides all the services I would ordinarily need, and more: I have discovered three first-rate restaurants and a half dozen others serving palatable food. There is little noise, and the notion that condominium development inevitably brings a horrid bustle in its train has here been met with a stiff rebuke. One reason is that the zoning board has outlawed the construction of buildings rising higher than four stories. The island is not merely a glorified hospice for rheumatic stockbrokers, as Florida coastal developments are often presumed to be. In addition to the condominiums there are a fair number of single houses, and there is an air of community around the place. Yet it resembles a traditional town no more than a street violinist resembles Isaac Stern. It stands instead as one more alternative to city life. There are others. One example is the proliferating mobile home. Another is the apartment complex built into the woods. The cities are being deliberately avoided for reasons unrelated to expense; in fact, with the exception of New York, Washington, San Francisco and maybe a couple of other places, it is cheaper to live inside the city than in the suburbs.

As the commitment to this manner of living increases, more careful attention is given to it. The lakeshores and seashores all over the country are vigilantly watched for signs of excessive and disorderly development. The residents become fussier about maintaining their communities, although, as I say, they are communities of a sort unknown to an earlier era.

The revolt against traditional urbanity is more strikingly observed in the development of shopping malls. At their inception in the 1950s these were miserable structures, squat and utterly without charm. The ruins of the early shopping centers can be seen today in suburban outposts, where steadily they have been abandoned by their customers and by the retailers who settled there to do business. They resemble the shopping malls being built today as a Model T Ford resembles a current Lincoln Continental. They have little in common besides parking lots. Shopping in the older centers was a matter of getting in, making a purchase, and getting out. There was no more joy in the experience than in kissing the face of the late Nikita Khrushchev. The newer shopping malls are infinitely more admirable. With their rolling aisles, several levels of stores, sunlit interiors and small cafés, there is the promise of something interesting: of rushing humanity, drawn from the surrounding communities, of chance meetings with old acquaintances, of the opportunity to observe people in the midst of saying something precious or preposterous.

My own hours inside these newfangled malls have often been amusing. I offer, as a specimen, the Fairlane Town Center outside of Detroit. Fairlane epitomizes the contemporary mall: not only is it distinctively designed, it is also connected to a gaudy Hyatt-Regency hotel by a monorail. Thousands enter and leave the place daily; many do not even bother to shop, but merely wander through, looking at windows, stopping for sugared refreshment, or sitting on benches. Some even go ice skating. On any given day a great cross-section of American humanity will present itself: Farmer Boob, just arrived in his pickup truck from Livingston County to buy his first polyester leisure suit, his wife at his side informing him how nice it is that he is "getting with it" at last . . . Mr. E. J. Banal, vice president of the Ford Motor Company, strolling into a shoe store to order his twelfth consecutive pair of cordovan brogues, and looking forward to his wife's compliment upon his arrival home . . . Miss Ernestina Crud, sitting happily in a corner, holding her third son in one hand and a chocolate chip cookie in the other, both of them financed by the United States Government . . . George Meek, assistant manager of a camera store, on his lunch break, rolling his eyes at Kathy Cupcake, chief of lingerie sales at J. C. Penney's, each wondering if that new shampoo has made the difference . . . Oliver Oodle, bad dude from Mack Avenue, feeling flush after a good week with the numbers, taking a long look at Ernestina Crud and deciding in the negative . . . Mrs. Nellie Fishface of Canton Township, eagerly examining the pale checked housedresses in Sears and wondering when they will go on sale . . . Tony Tonedeaf, manager of a jeans store, unbuttoning his shirt to the navel and turning up the volume on the store's stereo unit as a girl with dyed blonde hair enters . . . Kurt Clearinghouse, ace salesman with an impressive Hungarian accent, informing a woman buying a twenty-five-dollar handbag that it is made of genuine Persian calf; she, believing him, wondering silently if Scheherazade would have gone for it . . . in brief, a place as fascinating in its way as an Arabic bazaar. I am sure that there are dozens like it across the land. They draw people out from the cities and in from the surrounding countryside; they mark the commercial center of the metropolis, and no man who desires to understand his country can avoid them. I have weaved through Fairlane at least a hundred times, and have marched up and down New York's Madison Avenue as often. I make no effort to compare the quality of the shopping, but I proclaim the experience of the mall to be vastly more interesting. America's intellectuals have not yet hymned the shopping mall, because it is all too obviously a venture in pure capitalism, and thus unworthy of anything but their withering disdain. And yet within the past decade it has taken its place among the most significant institutions of the Republic. But it is no more an aspect of city life than of country life; such categories are superseded there.

The recent history of great sports arenas has similarly reflected the general willingness to avoid the old cities. Traditionally, a ball park has been to an American city as a cathedral is to a city in Europe. Tiger Stadium was the only genuine temple of my boyhood; the grand synagogue into which I was heaved on Saturday or Sunday mornings could not rival the subtlety of its aromas, the resonance of its sounds, the vesperish quality of a doubleheader's second game when Whitey Ford was pitching for the Yankees. Fortunately the place still stands, and I am able to vent all my religious instincts in a box behind the first-base dugout. But elsewhere people have not been so fortunate. Ball clubs have been removed to vast, comfortable but flavorless structures in the outlying regions; this has happened to Detroit's football team, which now plays its games in an unprofitable domed facility located in the fastnesses of Pontiac Township. Changes of this sort subtly affect people's attitudes toward their regions of residence. As a Detroiter I can sense the difference for myself: there is enormous psychological difference between viewing a sporting event at a great old stadium permeated with the sweat of the city's past, and at some dull new facility in the sticks without any history built into its refreshment stands. As with the population of woodsy apartments and the proliferation of the new shopping malls, the American is removed one step further from the city life to which he had never completely adjusted.

After all, it remains the case, as I have said, that the American will typically avoid identifying himself as a city man. Ask him what pleasures he would pursue if awarded time and leisure by the powers at hand, and he will not tell you that he would spend his hours perusing Tintorettos at the local art museum, or listening to Bach cantatas as rendered by the finest choir and chamber orchestra in the region, or attending ball games, or feasting at the finest restaurant in town. He will say that, given his choice, he will go to the mountains and start schussing, or survey some stream for trout, or proceed to the lake or ocean and unfurl his sails, or fire bullets at blameless deer, or lift his golf clubs from a rack and beat a small white ball over a few miles of tidy pasture. When he thinks of a sublime moment, he does not picture himself sitting in on a performance of *Hamlet* with Sir Laurence Olivier in the title role; he sees himself near some mountain or body of water, staring wonderingly at the moon, with a beloved individual close at hand. I have met Germans who work themselves into a nearly erotic enthusiasm at the prospect of attending the Bayreuth Festival; I have never met similar Americans, although I know many who love the music of Wagner, and would be pleased to attend. And I suppose that my own attitude falls into line with that of my countrymen. Something in our collective character causes us to pause before this total submission to civilization and its artifacts.

Yet, however much he fancies that his is the soul of a great outdoorsman, the American would seldom really choose a country life for himself. His pining after nature derives partially from honest restlessness, and partially from sentimental posturing. Thomas Jefferson was quite wrong to suppose that the true republic would be an American Arcadia, with every man farming for his own food, reading good deist literature by night, and meeting his neighbors for heartfelt discussions about the condition of the crops. Even as Jefferson dreamed, the weeds of urbanity, called bankers and lawyers, were covering the landscape, and there was no reason to suppose they would be easily supplanted. The current chaos in styles of living was not really unpredictable. True, a man of the early nineteenth century might not have believed that the America of the late twentieth century would attain fabulous wealth and yet would tolerate cities which were idiotically constructed and insanely governed. But of course he would not have counted on the mass-produced automobile, which changed everything.

I myself grow more sanguine on the subject as one year chases another away. As a city man by birth and temperament, I have naturally tended to line up with the angry intellectual mobs who demand that the cities of America be saved, lest the barbarians overrun the landscape. But I feel the certainty passing out of me, a sort of indifference moving in to replace it. Among the greatest talents of Americans is their ability to create fresh amusements which merge an intriguing strangeness with an appalling banality. So it is with modes of existence. It is often worthwhile to watch the show for a bit before choosing sides, which is what I shall do with the current update on Jefferson's dream: a contest between a civilization focused on its cities, and one in which cities are but incidental properties.

III.   NEW YORK DIRGES
AND CALIFORNIA DREAMS

Any consideration of this war in national behavior might as well include a look at the two symbols of the rival factions: New York City and the coastal region of the state of California. New York, in this scheme, is the biggest and wickedest of cities, encompassing the greatest glories and the deepest degradations in the American urban experience. It is a town which calls up legends at the mention of its name; those who celebrate it and those who denounce it concur in the belief that there is no place to match it. California, on the other hand, is the citadel of easy and glamorous living, blessed by nature. Its merits and defects are less sharply defined than those of New York, and as a consequence are less hotly debated. Nevertheless there is widespread belief that California is different from the rest of the country. Its temperate climate and position at the end of the continent provide partial explanation for this belief in California's distinctiveness. But far more important has been the establishment of the movie, television and popular recording industries in the southern part of the state.

Further north, San Francisco has advertised itself as a kind of American urban paragon, combining physical pleasantness with heroic advances in the art of living. Its inhabitants often believe that their superiority as representatives of humanity is ensured by their residency there. Indeed, this strange presumption also characterizes New Yorkers and Southern Californians, unlike citizens elsewhere in America,* thus contributing to the rivalry between New

* A notable exception is Texas, a state filled with boring braggarts. Another is the District of Columbia, which is resplendent with powerful bores.

York and California. But it is most noticeable among San
Franciscans, as their city, for all its supposed greatness,
boasts no more really distinguished residents than Cleveland, Ohio, and may even have fewer first-rate figures inside it than Houston, Texas, or Atlanta, Georgia. The city
instead thrives on a reputation as a haven for fourth-rate
poetry movements, idiotic schemes for self-improvement,
and homosexuals with angry voices pitched at their highest
levels. There is probably more senseless violence in the history of the town than in the history of any city in America.
Even in the seemlier circles of San Francisco, civilized life
is characterized by little more than a sort of blank-faced
mellowness. Such mellowness is greatly overrated. Those
who cite it as evidence of San Francisco's superiority are of
the same ilk as the people who equate chivalry with medie-
val civilization, and regard Chartres Cathedral as an artis-
tic sideshow to the main event; or those who recall pow-
dered wigs instead of Voltaire when they are asked to recall
something notable about the eighteenth century.

Between New York and California, I am unques-
tionably better acquainted with the big city on the East
Coast. As a literary man I have found it useful to spend
much of my time there in recent years, enhancing my fortune by withstanding the efforts of publishers to swindle
and oppress me. I have even, for the past two years, kept
an apartment on the island of Manhattan, maintaining
open house for the cockroaches and sewer rats of the neighborhood. As a man whose reputation is slight by New
York's greasy standards, and whose expense account is
nonexistent, I have moved freely in low circles as well as
high. My acquaintances include a feminist editor who
dresses in slept-in flannel work shirts when taking me to
lunch; a vendor of Nova Scotia salmon who hails me as
"maestro" and slices off a bit of his thumb with the salmon;

an aging, bewhiskered merchant of picture frames who subscribes to the hallucinatory pishposh of Aldous Huxley; a grocer, aged fifty, who has lived all his life in New York City, dreaming of attending a World Series but never attempting to purchase a ticket; a black lady author of advanced years and Roman faith, who wishes she could be the Pope; and dozens of other characters, many of them even more dubious than myself, including a depressing array of editors and agents.

I have caught the scent of the city's garbage on summer mornings. I have swerved to avoid defecating poodles on Madison Avenue. I have been jostled on East Eighty-sixth Street, sworn at on West Forty-second Street, and purred at on Christopher Street. I have dined around the corner from Park Avenue and sampled shish kebab on Ninth Avenue. I have witnessed Polish dancing inside Central Park. I have suffered Indian cooking in Yorkville. I have heard Puerto Ricans gabbing everywhere. I have seen my book displayed in the front window of Fifth Avenue stores. I have seen my book slaughtered by an idiot in the columns of the New York *Times*. I have survived Harlem at dusk. I have survived the babbling of publishers at midday. I have survived the view of Queens from Carl Schurz Park. In brief, New York has become my second home. It has long been so with many of the literati. This is not necessarily because writers love the town; indeed, hardly a single first-rate American author of the twentieth century has called New York his home for more than a brief spell. But the city is the center of publishing, and writers gravitate toward New York for reasons of commercial convenience. Once these commercial interests are served, it is common for writers to move along and settle themselves elsewhere. Some never bother to move to New York at all. Hemingway never lived there, and never cared for the town.

Faulkner lent himself to the Greenwich Village experience for a few months in his early twenties, and found it so unappetizing that he was reinstalled in Mississippi before he even attempted writing novels. The cases of H. L. Mencken and Eugene O'Neill are even more striking. Mencken kept his residence in Baltimore all his life, although during much of it he edited magazines in New York which required him to commute every third week. And O'Neill, the greatest man in the history of the American theater, spent remarkably little time in this supposed theatrical capital, once his head had cleared after the drinking bouts of his youth.

In other words, the American writer of the first rank has almost gone out of his way to avoid living in New York, particularly if he is not a native of the city. There are indubitably many writers living there, more of them than in any other town in America. But they are writers of the second, third, and fourth rank—and of the great and ghastly beyond. The typical New York writer is a journalistic jobber who enjoys receiving invitations to publishers' parties. He is an Alfred Kazin or Irving Howe, academics raised in the city's slums and ever dazzled by all the bright lights. He is a critic of dim talent and gray style—an Andrew Sarris, say, or one of the interchangeable dunces on the staff of the New York *Times*. He is a former screenwriter preparing to write novels, or a mediocre novelist stirring his drink inside Elaine's as he seeks consolation from his friends before heading to the "intellectual wasteland" of Hollywood. Or, increasingly, "he" is a "she," angry at the injustices of the isms of America, with a bitterly ironic smile pushing protests from her lips as she plots out her next novel.

The reason behind this state of affairs is not hard to find. Simply, it is this: for all its vast showiness, New York

offers no anchor to the writer, and so unless he is seduced
by the fumes, bad manners and high rents of the city, he
might as well live in a smaller town. There is no "New
York intellectual life," as neglected fools often suppose;
there is only a fair scattering of hunt-and-peck artists, some
of whom happen to know each other. Whatever influence
emanates from such circles is rarely worth mentioning.
There is also the company of publishers, but this resembles
the company of in-laws: best if minimized.

Indeed, the power of New Yorkers in various areas of
life has been greatly exaggerated. The city is admittedly
supreme in a few of the arts, but they are those arts whose
vitality has lagged and which have tended as a result to
consolidate themselves inside a single town. One example is
serious music, which has steadily declined since the glorious days of the nineteenth century. The symphony orchestra or opera house of our day is little more than a performing museum; occasional introductions of new works are
little better than lip services paid to the grand tradition.
The rise of dance as an almost cultlike enthusiasm of
civilized people is symptomatic of the general state of the
musical arts. Reading the musical press of the day, one is
momentarily lulled into the presumption that a Balanchine
or some other choreographic magnifico ought to be regarded as the creative equal of a Brahms, or even a Men-
delssohn. Within a decade it will be possible for a discrim-
inating concertgoer not to know the name of a single living
composer—and not to care.

Another example is painting—in fact, all the still and
silent visual arts. The New Yorker, sipping spritzers in the
galleries up and down Madison Avenue and in the smelly
old warehouses of Soho, can convince himself that these
are heady days in the history of painting and sculpture.
Artsy ladies from Kansas City can fly into town for long

weekends spent in contemplation of the latest wonder, before reporting back to their sisters in the flatlands. Nervous critics with food-stained beards can weave wonderful theories of Neo-Blobism. Everyone can assure himself that the philistines are fifty years behind the times, and that the "Footprints in Oil" by Henry Hocus-Pocus will some day rival the nude bathers of Renoir in the affections of the public. But such excitement is atavistically inspired: because these have been great arts in the past, goes the assumption, they must be great today. Observers with more severe and sensible critical temperaments will admit that the camera may well have dealt these arts a mortal blow by robbing them of their primary raison d'être.

Finally, consider the theater, for ages the most democratic of all arts, with its requirement of an audience. Here, too, New York has lorded it over the rest of the country. The thrill of a visit to New York was often described in terms of one's opportunity to experience theatrical delights. Despite the growth of regional theaters in recent decades, this has not changed much. But what of it? Not since the days when Puritans were disturbing the peace by running around denouncing theaters as dens of depravity has the theater been of less consequence to the cultural life of the Republic. Interesting new plays are produced from time to time, but there has not been anything really first-rate in decades. Even if there had been, it would have no more effect on the state of civilization in America than the unearthing of a forgotten lyric by William Cullen Bryant. A passion for theater begins to resemble a passion for contemporary lyric poetry: an innocent and perhaps beneficial eccentricity of minor importance. The young actor will still make the journey to New York, enduring an apprenticeship of waiting on tables and playing Rosencrantz for no fee in drafty churches. Some theatrical experience is still expected of him. But New York is the minor league for an actor today. He will flee to California at the first opportunity, as he knows his fortune is to be made there. Playwrighting is still being done, but the vocation of playwrighting is supplanted by the vocation of screenwriting. Even the jolly boulevardiers who gave the theater its cheap vitality have gone west with their joke bags: witness Neil Simon, the most fabulously successful of them all, notwithstanding his partial return to the city which raised him and carried him to fame on its shoulders. Such things simply did not happen in the past, when theatrical culture was a going concern.

The New Yorker and the New Yorkophile are understandably reluctant to face the implications of these developments. But the city's claim to be the capital of American culture has less legitimacy now than at any time in the past. Perhaps preeminence would never have slipped away if New York had also been the political capital. The situation of New York was never in any case really analogous to that of London and Paris, as has often been supposed. The sheer size of America had as much to do with this as the fact of Washington, D.C. The United States has in this respect been similar to Germany. At any given time there have been a half dozen German cities of general significance; there are at least as many in the United States. The decline of New York's importance in American life has been mitigated by its seeming elevation in international status. The installation of the United Nations promised much glory to the city. Also there has been an assortment of refugees, many of them prosperous, settling in the town to escape the exhaustion and economic instability of European life. But whatever Europeanization of American life has occurred is due to the vast numbers of Americans who have traveled abroad since the Second World War. The United Nations, meanwhile, has firmly established itself as the Parliament of Idiocy, and no man of any sense pays the slightest attention to its doings, save for purposes of occasional low comic relief from daily cares. The movement of foreigners into New York has in other words done nothing to enhance life in the United States, and may not even have enhanced life in New York City itself.

I make these observations without joy. As a city man I would have preferred that New York appear in our time as the dazzling epitome of urban life, as bewitching to all seekers of fortune as the Paris of Balzac or the London of Dickens—or even the London of Dr. Johnson, worthy of refurbishing his claim that when one is tired of such a city, one is tired of life. But it simply is not so. New York can still intimidate with its size, impress with its noise and delight with its amusements. But these are the hollow intimidations, impressions and amusements of the mere headquarters town. The mark of a genuine capital is its capacity to embody the life of the nation at large, raised to exponential levels. No one could seriously make such a claim for New York. Wherever it performs as a capital—in the arts of music, painting, theater—the issues are no longer vital. Otherwise it is merely a place where deals are made. Its status as the financial center of the nation is beyond dispute, but this gives it no more claim to first place among American cities than Frankfurt would have among German cities on the basis of its position in that republic. Ultimately New York's pretensions to imperial dignity resemble the similar pretensions of the late King Farouk of Egypt: they are composed of mere grossness and gaudiness, and are no more solid than his three hundred pounds of fat. The city is far less singular than is generally supposed; its boosters and detractors credit it far too heavily with properties it does not possess. Even its crime problem is unremarkable. At least a dozen other American cities can claim as much depravity per capita. And as the high-rise boxes proliferate along New York's avenues—skyscrapers without any of the piercing appeal of the Chrysler and Empire State buildings of yesteryear—the city evolves into one of the most hideous on earth.

Of late, Washington, D.C., has come to be regarded with much of the same fascinated suspicion that has in the past attached itself to life in New York. This has been due to the growth of federal budgets. People tend to suppose that wherever there is evidence of much money floating around, there must also be all sorts of eerie and elegant doings. The columns of Mr. Jack Anderson help to reinforce this suspicion by exposing official arrogance, which seems invariably to reveal itself in "posh" and "plush" settings. But the attempt to create a mystique around life in Washington has been seriously hampered by a series of remarkably dull Presidents of the United States. In Washington the mechanized chatter of a Kennedy passes for genuine wit; the low, incompetent schemings of a Nixon pass for high drama; the State of the Union addresses of a Carter pass for oratory. It is all unconvincing; where the most glorified among our glorious leaders is so very uninteresting, it is hard to imagine that the excitement of life in Washington can be anything worth yelling about. Of course this could change; the potential for a democratic Versailles exists. If ever the citizens of these States elect as their leader a man who bursts spontaneously into Shakespearean soliloquies or lets rumors float about his taste for the great-great-granddaughters of slaves, then watch the fashionable folk rush into town. New York will assume a ghostly aspect at such a time, and people will regard its affairs with no more interest than they currently regard the affairs of Calcutta or São Paolo.

In the meantime, most of the nation's leering is

directed at California. In the old days the westward adventurer was enticed by rumors of gold; in more recent times the enticements have been detailed in terms of exceptionally pleasant weather, extraordinarily beautiful specimens of humanity, and notable progress in the arts of living. These conditions supposedly obtain in all of coastal California; in the San Francisco Bay Area, a kind of intellectual excitement is also supposed to prevail. What of these claims? The superiority of California weather, to those who disdain extreme cold, is undeniable. The beauty of the state's citizens may well be enhanced by sun-tanning, although this process has rarely been decisive in transforming toads into princesses. The Bay Area's intellectual excitement appears, however, to be of a wholly bogus order, as I remarked earlier. There is no more reason to presume the advance of civilization in San Francisco than to presume it in Mr. Gerald Rafshoon's essays in presidential promotion. The Berkeley campus of the University of California developed a reputation for particularly tasty radicalism which may have been unwarranted in the first place, and is certainly so today. In any case the state ought to provide Mr. Mario Savio with an annual pension in recognition of his permanent contribution to California tourism.

This leaves the state of the arts of living as the most curious and challenging of California's claims. Although I would certainly prefer wiggling my toes in the Southern California sun to slogging through the streets of Detroit on most February afternoons, I am yet struck by the transparency of this claim. The California life is personified by someone called a star, who passes his days amid a luxuriance of palm trees and swimming pools. A star is some sort of successful performer: actor, joke teller, rock singer —it doesn't much matter as long as he is successful. The lives of stars are made familiar to the public by a variety of journals, ranging from *Esquire* and *Rolling Stone* to the *National Enquirer* and *Teen Beat*. The star is also likely to appear as a guest on television talk shows, on which he chats about this or that, incidentally sketching in the viewer's mind a picture of California life. The American is thus able to imagine himself more familiar with the appearance, tastes and habits of his favorite stars than with the appearance, tastes and habits of his Uncle Arthur in Altoona, Pa., or of the appearance, tastes and habits of the Vice President of the United States.

This is significant because, invariably, the tastes and habits of stars are very vulgar. After all, these are men and women who, in other civilized generations, were regarded as the social equals or inferiors of prostitutes, bootblacks and usurers. In these cultivated democratic territories, however, they are exalted as artists of the first order, creative beings, political experts, humanity's brightest flowers. Even among the intelligentsia, the name of Brando is whispered as if it were Bach. As one who has witnessed a great many bad performances of various kinds, I can appreciate talent as much as the next man, but there can be no doubt that performers as a breed are among the most spectacularly overrated creatures in current civilization. In fairness to our times, it should be noted that the people of the nineteenth century seem not to have been intrinsically better in this respect. Tolstoy, for example, once depicted the Russians swooning over Sarah Bernhardt at a point in her career when she was no more divine than Mamie Eisenhower. But the incessant intimacy of television and the chronic circulation of popular journals have transformed this situation into a kind of unstoppable mania. It is practically impossible for a man to live an active life in the United States and remain unaware of who the stars happen to be.

The effects of this on the great majority of Americans

are obvious. Consider the case of Joe Joiner, class of '62, now married with two children and serving the Republic by promising justice to the abandoned wives of construction workers in Aurora, Illinois. Joe's law practice is successful enough, but how can Joe measure his success against that of his old friend John Joyful, also class of '62, and the star of a television series called "Pork and Pinky," concerning the hijinks of a private detective firm in which one sleuth is male, and the other, female? Tonight Joe is at home with his family, watching his old friend sit in a Southern California television studio and describe to the world how, last week, he birdied the same hole that had been bogeyed by a fellow member of his foursome, the Hon. Gerald R. Ford.

Now, although Joe and his family think—let us give them credit, and say they *know*—that John is a no more distinguished character than Joe, they cannot help finding the situation itchy. It is too much to expect Joe and his family merely to accept this state of affairs as predetermined. Why, after all, has Joe not been marked out to play golf with former Presidents, and discuss the results on national television? Now Joe, his wife and kids do not necessarily believe that any of them are actors with the talent of John Joyful, nor do they resent his success. But they naturally wonder, each in his own way, why they should not be closer to this place where eminence is so easily attained, and where in any case the weather is so nice. And so, if the itch is strong enough, they pick themselves up and move, and if it is not so strong, they retain their fascination with the possibilities of California life; perhaps one of the kids will move out there some day.

So it is interesting to consider the American in the context of the myths that drive him onward. If a young writer travels to New York, stands beneath the Washington Square Arch, looks up Fifth Avenue and vows silently that he will conquer the city, it may safely be assumed that he has read Balzac and Thomas Wolfe too literally, that he takes himself too seriously, and that he is due for a rude awakening. This is not because he is necessarily untalented, or even less than great. But his dreams will not be met because they are irrelevant to the situation: New York literary life is far blander and less important than he supposes, and if fame comes to him, it will do so in unexpected ways. Similarly, the Californian's conviction that there is magic in the air around him becomes in itself an important aspect of his life. How many Americans exist whose life histories can be told in terms of the unraveling of early fantasies? I do not presume to speculate, and the Census Bureau is preoccupied with other matters. And so this most interesting statistic will go unrecorded.

IV. THE DECLINE OF OLD DIXIE

In the social imagination of the nation, no development has exceeded in importance the decline of the old rivalry between North and South. Still in its early stages, its effects will remain unclear for some time yet. Popular notions of the South as an especially romantic territory are by no means completely dead, although they survive mainly in the minds of women who buy wretched historical novels. These books concern southern belles of the Civil War period who sacrifice their virtue to the passion of northern soldiers with fire in their eyes. The woman who reads this stuff is likely to be herself a Northerner, and she might even, after artful questioning, admit that the period described in the books is quite dead, and that the South was never really all that glorious. But deep down she prefers to believe that southern life was as lusty as the books describe, and that at least some of this lustiness is alive in the South today. Then, too, there are southern women who pretend to keep alive the tradition of the southern belle, and strut about as they believe ladies strutted about during the presidency of Jefferson Davis. No man of any sense, however, pays much attention to them, and only morons marry them.

The southern male is unlikely to revert to such ancient form except, occasionally, after the college football bowl games are played on New Year's Day. Whenever the University of Alabama wins the Sugar Bowl game and yet fails to receive top ranking in the subsequent polls of coaches and sportswriters, Southerners start denouncing the blameless wire services as instruments of a Yankee conspiracy attempting to punish them for seceding from the Union.

This resurgent Rebel pride must, however, be accounted exceptional. With the relaxation of the racial codes which used to prevail in the South, Northerners and Southerners are more comfortable with each other. Indeed, the Southerner's superior sense of courtesy may even give him an edge in casual relations. The Northerner is less likely to drive through Mississippi fearing potbellied sheriffs with police dogs at their side. If he is caught in some speed trap, as is likely, he may have the consolation of being arrested by a black sheriff. The Southerner, in his turn, may now wander through northern cities with full confidence that he has been preceeded by such distinguished and well-loved representatives of the New South as the Reverend Billy Graham, Mr. Billy Carter, or Miss Dolly Parton. The political scene too is greatly changed, with the retirement of such wonderful advocates of states' rights as Senator James O. Eastland and Governor George C. Wallace, and with the concurrent rise of Jimmy Carter to eminence. All this has contributed to a jumbling of images.

I must say that I view these developments with some

ambivalence. I am only an intermittent champion of progress, which tends to claim too large a portion of life's
charm and color in working its will. It is good that there
are no more lynchings in the South, and that blacks are
now free to attend state universities without being thought
heroic for doing so. But the image of the Dark and Dangerous South was as attractive to Northerners as the image of
Darkest Africa has been to Western Europeans for several
generations. Also this image served an important national
purpose: here within the borders of the Republic was a situation so strikingly repulsive that every American had a legitimate outlet for the moral indignation which wells up
within him as surely as the smell of herring fills the air
around a Lithuanian fishmonger. Here, too, was an irrefutable check on the American's boast that he lived in the
most civilized of countries—in the greatest nation in the
history of the world, as he is often so pleased to say.

Now all this has been confounded. I have no idea
whether the United States is the greatest nation in the history of the world. I *do* profoundly hope that a country
whose most admired citizens include wealthy joke tellers,
evangelical crusaders against homosexuals, and the wife of
any President of the United States, is *not* the most civilized
nation on earth. I prefer to believe that there may be better
places elsewhere, and that, if I behave myself, I will get to
see them. The trouble with racial progress is that it encourages smugness. Americans may feel that the state of their
civilization is better than ever, and that the foreigner is
without legitimate cause for serious complaint about the
country. When Solzhenitsyn denounced the condition of his
adopted home at a recent Harvard commencement, his recitation was admittedly crude, but in all the critical reviews
of his performance, there was little effort made to sort out
his comments in the light of Western history over the past

few centuries. Everyone was instead content to compare Solzhenitsyn's limited perceptions of the United States with his broader and deeper perspectives of the Soviet Union which had exiled him. It was as if the United States and Russia, as the two primary political powers of the era, were the only places capable of significant attainments or failures in the world today. Europe, a pleasant enough little continent, no longer really counted for much. As the Soviet Union is little more than a grotesque caricature of civilized life, the United States seems in this scheme an obvious paragon; whatever happens here must necessarily be the best or at any rate the most important thing that could happen anywhere.

The cleanup of the racial problem removes the stigma from such presumption. But the response of the civilized man is to pause and wonder about the value of this development. Because he is civilized, he is not necessarily unhappy in America; the nature of civilized men is to cultivate the territory around them, and they are miserable only if hampered in their efforts. Because he is left fairly free to pursue his interests in America, he cannot complain in this regard. Yet, like Solzhenitsyn, he has his sensitivities assaulted daily by the things he sees and hears all around him. The boasts of national greatness ring hollow in his ears, and he is inclined to critical demurrers. Many of the advances in American life seem somehow beside the point. He must consider whether a Carter constitutes a genuine improvement over a Sam Ervin; whether the crooners of Nashville, Tennessee, are really a greater gift to the nation than the creators of the Negro spirituals. I do not argue that he decides one way or the other; I say only that he must give the matter some thought.

3

Memories of
Public Education

I. OF PEDAGOGY, AND THE
PEDAGOGY OF PEDAGOGY

If I were a pretender to thoroughness, and determined to paint either a complete self-portrait or a broader sketch of the times, I would raise the issue of parents and families and deal with it at length. This is because family life remains by far the most overwhelming influence on individual life.

But the mood for such considerations is not upon me and I shall pass on to a subject which, in these great States, is widely supposed to be at least as important as the subject of families. If not exactly the opium of free peoples, public education is still a fairly strong drug, injected into society with fervent expectations for its success. It is generally assumed that the process of schooling, with a little help from parents, will manage to create acceptable citizens and keep this nation great and free. My own conviction is that in this equation, families count for at least 75 per cent and schools for no more than 25 per cent if the procedural burdens are properly borne—but I shall not enter into argument over these relative burdens, and shall pass promptly to the subject of educators.

The average educator, after all, is but a slight improvement on an ignoramus. He is able to run a fair amount of information through his system, which gives him an edge on the rest of the citizenry, but he is rarely capable of digesting it, which keeps the edge slight. Occasionally one runs across a schoolteacher who is mad about his subject and reads a half dozen books about it every month, but this is as rare and as startling as meeting up with a state legislator who looks at himself in the mirror each morning and vows to perform at least one public service in the coming day. The average schoolteacher is instead preoccupied with an ideal of pedagogy that he has carried within him since collegiate days. All sorts of bogus controversies have been generated by the schools of education, dealing in the trivial areas with which the mind of the professional educator manages to busy itself. Not a single educational study, for example, has attempted to establish that the number of first-rate minds or characters turned out of public schools today is greater than, say, thirty years ago. Yet the issue is far more significant than whether or not more youths with dark skin are earning diplomas. The fact of the diploma is uninteresting beside the question of whether the diploma has been acquired by reading *Hamlet* with admiration and endeavoring to grasp the principles of the American Civil War, or by declaiming the lyrics of Nikki Giovanni and absorbing the political views of Paul Robeson. And so such studies are invariably hollow and insignificant.

Whatever credit educators take for the future achievement of students cannot help but be rather dubious. The graduate of Lincoln Junior High who grows up to invent a new vaccine against swine flu is no more an example of the excellence of Lincoln Junior High than a Jimmy Carter is proof of the high state of civilization in rural Georgia.

The most interesting thing about schools of education is the fact of their existence. One would not at first consider the pedagogical art as something lending itself to vast instruction—a course here and there in child and adolescent psychology, certainly; a few moments given over to detailing the infinite uses of blackboards, certainly; a lecture on the technique of grading, no doubt useful. But the prospective schoolteacher spends 25 per cent of his time in his last two years of college learning about education.

Many teachers denounce the hours wasted in these education classes, and recall their bouts with the theories of professors of education as the rest of us remember campfires at which the principal activity was the swatting of mosquitoes. With an occasional exception, the actual theories of the professors have little impact on the work of schoolteachers; mainly this is due to their irrelevance to classroom situations. Fundamentally, after all, the reason for sending children to school is similar to the reason for domesticating cats: it is better than listening to them go shrieking through the alleys. And yet there are few schoolteachers, good or bad, who do not imagine that they are engaged in a noble task: the creation of souls. It is this belief which supports the schools of education, and permits them to sustain the delusion that the teaching of education is analogous to the teaching of law, or medicine, or engineering. And so the schoolteacher, whether he finds educational theory useful or not, will suspect that teaching is in itself a greater enterprise than history, English or mathematics, and that his first professional loyalty is to an ideal of teaching, rather than to the accumulated wisdom of historians, poets and mathematicians. The school of education is thereby enshrined as the temple of schoolteachers, embodying the sort of holy irrelevance which is implied in the roles of churches everywhere in these righteous and protestant States.

So schoolteaching wavers between being a kind of high-salaried babysitting and an instrument for moral instruction. It is axiomatic in America that anything useful will have its usefulness exaggerated, and so education has been sniffed out and chased by the ideological hounds. There are those on one side who can be counted on to stop just short of tears in regretting that education, as "the great equalizer" of American life, has failed dreadfully to realize its potential, and those on the other side who affect grave concern that restraints on prayer at the start of the school day are hastening America's downfall. Behind these factions are various groups of timorous parents, often represented on oafish boards of education, who are eager to discover scapegoats if their children turn out badly.

Yet all this amounts to a preposterous overestimation of the importance of education in people's lives. The pure-faced and the pimpled attend school in the same state of nature in which despairing pedagogues have always found them—mindful of their arms and legs in early years, concerned for their hormonal activity as they grow older, and incorrigibly resistant to the idea of having their minds taxed and thus having their attention diverted from more active concerns.

Of course there are exceptions, but even so it is difficult to find a man of the first rank who willingly credits his early schoolteachers with a serious role in his development. Sentimental recollections abound: one can track down great writers whose family lives have been unhappy and who have found compensation in the sympathy of their teachers. But this has nothing to do with education per se, and one's feeling upon reading of such kindly exercises is that the young genius would have fared as well if he had happened to be apprenticed to a clockmaker, or hired to shuffle medicine bottles for a nearsighted physician. One takes one's basic education where one finds it, and after a time native talent will assert itself. Imagine Shakespeare's spelling teacher claiming the tiniest bit of credit for *Hamlet!* Or Jefferson's Bible tutor insisting that he helped to inspire the Declaration of Independence! Think of the fellow who first whispered "Nietzsche" into the ears of Thomas Mann trying to convince scholars of his contribution to *The Magic Mountain!* Consider these things, laugh hard for a minute, and then give sober thought to the question of the educator's business. Of course, in time, a first-rate mind will find other first-rate minds in its chosen field—a Beethoven will get hold of the best counterpoint teacher around, a Shakespeare will hail a stage manager— but that is another matter altogether.

The educators themselves do not pretend to be laboring on behalf of an elite; as they readily and even enthusiastically point out, the purpose of mass education is to benefit the masses, and so it is hardly surprising that this adds up to little more than the provision of an anodyne for the mediocre. The surprising thing is that so much fuss is made about it. I happen to believe that anyone who reads the writings of educators seriously ought to forfeit his right to speak on any important matter before the Republic. Educational prose is the worst in the English language, and regular readings of it are clearly as harmful to the mind and body as the taking of poison. Anyone who indulges the habit of his own volition offers irrefutable evidence of his feeblemindedness, and ought to be treated accordingly. In my capacity as a social pathologist, I have myself examined educational prose on occasion, but only after receiving a series of thorough inoculations to combat the foul effects which would otherwise seize me after an hour's reading. I have penetrated far enough to discover that the American pedagogical theorist is mainly interested in finding some way to get the spirit of democracy into the classroom. There is a presumption that the democratic spirit is the upholstering of all worthy educational experience, and that the great educator functions as a kind of supreme democrat. Much of this wisdom has been warmed over and passed down from decade to decade since early in the century, when it was first presented to yawning audiences by Papa John Dewey. The schoolteachers who receive it are encouraged to believe that their work is a far more complicated and mysterious business than they might otherwise suppose. It is hard to say how many of them accept this belief for themselves.

My own experience as a waif in the wilderness of public schools, which ended a mere five years ago, led me to an opposite conclusion. The work of schools, properly done, is work of the utmost simplicity, involving the communication of information which the teacher has not thought about too rigorously. This neglect on the teacher's part is what makes his work so simple. He need only pass along something that he has been taught in his turn, and all the work is in discovering and employing the best means of communication. Most often this reduces to a question of discipline. And so the great debates of educators have reflected the tension between their commitment to invest schooling with as much of the democratic spirit as possible, and the natural despotism of classrooms.

At the end of the 1950s I was submitted to the publicly salaried educators of the city of Detroit. Many of them were spinsters of great age and temperament. They had matriculated in the first third of the century, and were nearing the end of their years of service. Later, by moving to the suburbs, I was able to compare these aged women with the newer breed of educators, freshly tenured and ready to uplift the youth of America with more modern techniques. Finally, I had the opportunity to taste of professorial delights at the University of Michigan, the oldest and most distinguished of all American state universities. And so throughout my educational career I was sitting in the catbird seat, as Mr. Red Barber used to say in another context: I was witness to the main developments and changes of the past quarter-century. Recalling those years now, they seem to have been one long and generally frustrated effort on the part of educators to get the attention of the young souls in their midst. It mattered little whether the subject matter was the isosceles triangle, the novels of Dickens, or the difference between igneous and sedimentary rocks. It was, in brief, one vast excuse for the metaphysical doodlings of professors of education.

II. CONCERNING COUNSELORS AND PRINCIPALS

The highest salaried and potentially most awesome figure in any American public school is the principal. After the principal and his assistants come the counselors, blessed with the majesty of their titles and the professional obligation to advise other people of their responsibilities—people too young to have the slightest idea of whether their counsel is right or wrong. To be sure, the principal and counselor are less likely to have more impact on the student's life than the lowly schoolteacher, but even so they are notable.

The woman who ruled over my Detroit elementary school was, for example, a singular personage in the students' eyes. She gave the school its tone, although none of us ever spoke to her. Teachers would threaten to send bothersome students to her office, and like any appeal to human fear of the unknown, this was effective. But such threats were never executed. Probably Miss R. had ordered that they not be. She was a woman of tremendous girth, whose days were passed almost entirely inside her office. The general hunch was that she spent much time eating. Only at the lunch hour would she emerge, straightening the jacket of her tight-fitting gray suit and strutting powerfully down the hall and into the lunchroom. There she proceeded directly to the head of any line that might have formed, and snatched two overflowing trays which had been set aside for her by the cooks. Then she would turn and retrace her steps, with all the students in the hallways standing aside to make way for her. Soon she would disappear into her office, not to be seen again until lunch hour of the following day. The two trays sometimes prompted attempts at humor among us: occasionally a boy would affect an imitation of Miss R.'s stirring strut, a scowl on his face and hand motions indicating her heaving bosom. Otherwise no efforts were made to satirize her imperial presence.

Surely this was as she wanted it. The school was sternly operated, and anyone who undertook mischief fully expected to be punished for it. Of course this did not even slightly reduce the amount of mischief undertaken by the students; like the incidence of homosexuality in the general population, it is a fairly constant factor from one generation to the next. Out in the suburbs, behavior was pretty much the same, although reaction to it was quite different. Instead of the inscrutable glutton of my early years, I discovered principals and administrators who were eager to meet with students and conduct conversations with them in the halls—pleasant ladies and gents, with an air of being at your service. One presumed their individuality, and yet chats with them followed a familiar pattern: How you doin'? Fine, Mr. X. Everything going all right with you this year? Just great, Mr. X. Glad to hear it—and off they would go. Occasionally one might try to steer a principal into more substantive areas of conversation, but this could cause further deterioration of the conversation. Asked for his views on some national affair of the recent past, one administrator told me he had been a typing teacher in those days, and so knew "no more about it than your parents." It is hard to say whether such people believe themselves shrewd psychologists in speaking with jovial disdain of their inability to understand "you kids," or if some native stupidity is at work.

The guidance counselor at a contemporary secondary school is an even more curious character. He lives in a world of his own creation, filled with immutable schedules and visions of completed course requirements. Some counselors have taken up their tasks after renouncing schoolteaching, while others have arrived at counseling in much the same way that their brothers and sisters in Christ landed in monasteries and nunneries—after hearing summonses from above.

The old-fashioned counselor projected superb confidence in the destiny of his students. There was one aging spinster who would schedule her seventh graders and then proceed with absolute certainty to mark out the educational careers of her students all the way through high school. If the mood was upon her, she would tell the seventh grader what his college major would be. This information was imparted in tones worthy of a great god, and so the seventh grader was inclined to accept it. The career of such a counselor must have been at least as pleasant as the career of a futurist: filled with great plans, and devoid of any requirement to check up on their fulfillment.

The younger counselor tends to be less majestic. He is a man or woman of middle age and smiling countenance, who has managed to elevate cheerful tolerance beyond the level of practical virtue, and has made it a fixed principle of conduct. Once the student is able to articulate his desires, the contemporary counselor will help him find the best way to achieve their realization. If the student tells his counselor that he wishes to study law, the counselor will comment that it is a grand ambition. If the student adds that he would like to defend criminals, the counselor will nod his head and reflect silently on the excellence of his institution, as indicated by the presence of such fine young people as this. Informed finally that the student wants most of all to defend terrorists, the counselor will naturally smile and comment that this is all very well, but it is necessary first to establish good grades in a sound prelaw program.

So the counselor is likely to be the softest creature around any school these days, just as the principal, for all his jolly airs, is apt to be the toughest. This is because the counselor is without very exact duties, while the administrator is forever haunted by his budgets. The individuals most representative of the state of education are still the schoolteachers, the foot soldiers in the army of the uplift.

III.   SERMONS AND SPITBALLS

The first business of the schoolteacher is to get the attention of his class; after that he must hold it. The nature of schooling in America is such that there is rarely time for grander achievements after these initial efforts have been undertaken. Occasionally one hears rumors of some Chicago Socrates or a Pied Piper of Pittsburgh, inspiring his flock to extraordinary peaks of human intelligence, but I am inclined to regard these in much the same way I regard reports of unidentified flying objects: as interesting possibilities of no immediate concern. The American schoolteacher begins as an idealist, but before long he is worrying about his tenure, in order to assure himself that he has retained his senses and was not a fool to enter such a profession. The magical theories of professors of education are bleakly exposed upon one's first contact with the magnificent indifference of student bodies. From the first, timid and useless efforts of the first-grade science teacher to gather the eyes of all "A students," to the last, dying fall of the American history professor attempting to liven things up with dreadful jokes, I recall nothing of schooling which was as significant as this: the struggle to arrest the attention of people whose interests lie elsewhere. This is as true of so-called intellectual students as of dumber specimens; the nature of intellectual students, after all, is to have an assortment of interests apart from schoolroom assignments, and, indeed, in conflict with them.

The spinsters and widows of my early years in Detroit included several notable disciplinarians. The librarian, for example, was a wrinkled woman of no more than one hundred pounds. Given her position as custodian of the school's intellectual treasures, she seemed remarkably ignorant. Although I was not in those days a great reader, I was, like everyone else, required to peruse a book during library class, and occasionally I would call upon her for advice. Once I asked her for a baseball biography and she handed me a football novel; another time I put in a request for Civil War history and was handed a Leatherstocking tale. This little lady was most interested in the exercise of power. Every five minutes during our assigned reading hour she would interrupt in her quavering voice, announcing that she had just discovered someone talking in a far corner of the library. This was about to be noted with her "trusty red pen," and the offender's grade would be suitably affected.

The shepherdess of my second-grade year was a woman of married title, though we always supposed she was a widow who had recaptured true bliss upon rejoining her chaste sisters in the schoolteaching sorority. She was a singularly round woman with an abbreviated neck who wore side-tie shoes. Sweat came naturally and freely to her face, and she engaged in memorable denunciations of classroom noise. The effectiveness of these tantrums was quite limited, however. She tended to run out of breath at the end of a heated paragraph, and yet she would continue mouthing indignant phrases after the wind power to make them audible had left her. This seemed rather funny to seven-year-olds, and after school we would imitate her and compare her to the fatter half of Abbott and Costello.

There was a first-grade teacher who was known as "the hag" because she had a fairly long nose, a couple of prominent warts, and dry gray hair tied into a bun at the back of her head. She could not grow angry without showering saliva on the first two rows of seats. But the hag was not the most repellent teacher in the school; nor was she the teacher to make the best use of her physical qualities. Both of these distinctions went to the woman who guided me through half of the third grade. Not merely old, she was badly put together, with unkempt hair, sad eyes, and sagging jowls adorned with protuberant white moles; worse, she dressed in dreadful sweaters, probably home-knit, with holes in them and musty smells about them. Her favored method of classroom discipline was to require offenders against silence to remain in their seats for one hour after the official end of the school day. Once, in a rare departure from my usual probity, I managed to get caught chatting and so was forced to submit to her punishment in the company of a doltish boy and a girl whom all boys disliked because she wore eyeglasses and so was presumed to be teacher's pet. This was her first offense, too, and had I not foolishly sinned that same day I would have spent the afternoon in the company of comrades who were undoubtedly celebrating this rupture in her reputation. Instead the three of us were left sitting at our desks. The novelty here derived from the teacher's refusal to assign us useless tasks on the order of copying "I will not talk in class" five hundred times. We were expected merely to sit there and, inevitably, look at the teacher. It was an extraordinary punishment; I was careful not to get caught again.

But the most memorable of all disciplinarians was my fifth-grade teacher, a widow in her fifties. Her instruction was barked in the mean accent of Appalachia, and after one of her more violent explosions, we would often huddle on the playground and circulate theories about the origin of her career. Most popular by far was the notion that she had murdered her husband in Kentucky and fled to Detroit, where, after an appropriate period of anonymity, she had taken up schoolteaching. This gave all of us the delicious sensation of living endangered lives as we entered the classroom each day. The natural bad temper of Mrs. V. was exacerbated by the fact that she saw and heard things poorly: her eyes were severely crossed and she wore an inefficient hearing aid. Often she strolled up and down the aisles to see if arithmetic problems were being solved. She never congratulated anyone for being correct, but she informed those who were in error by flicking the backs of their necks with her middle finger. This was more stunning than painful, but it certainly inspired everyone's best effort.

Mrs. V. was known as the only teacher in school who had no favorites among her students. This earned her a surprising amount of respect. Occasionally she would even holler at those quiet girls who wore eyeglasses, which roused the boys in class to their closest approximation of real enthusiasm for her. Usually, however, her victims came from the standard roster of young rogues who had been getting into trouble ever since kindergarten. Her most famous essay in repression was inspired by a rascal who had shaped his recently returned history test into a paper airplane and sent it flying directly to her desk. It landed on top of a pile of papers. Mrs. V. lifted it up and asked the boy, with poorly managed restraint, what he supposed he was doing. He responded coolly, "Isn't that the way the Wright brothers started?" Now totally enraged, Mrs. V. picked up her yardstick and stalked toward his desk. He had about three seconds in which to move, and he used only one of them. Presently she began to chase him around the room, yelling, "I'll get you, you little whippersnapper!" She held the yardstick high above her head, and moved with the limited grace and swiftness of one hampered by bad eyesight, a long dress, and general clumsiness. He kept his distance from her without the slightest difficulty. After two revolutions around the room, Mrs. V. was panting. She returned to her desk, told the offender to sit down, and ordered him to remain seated when the rest of the class was dismissed. Their meeting took place without an audience, but we learned that the rascal had been told his behavior was unacceptable, and he had promised to improve. He had won not only the battle, but apparently the war as well. Within a week he was back in trouble, but Mrs. V. left her yardstick alone and limited herself to calling him a whippersnapper. Her reputation as a disciplinarian continued to be formidable, however, and no one challenged her to the chase again.

That was my final year in the Detroit public schools. In the summer of 1964 my family repaired to the suburbs. There the old-fashioned disciplinarian could not survive unless there was an aspect of humor to his methods. I think of the eighth-grade American history instructor, at last report still active, who must objectively be accounted a terrible teacher. His ignorance of his subject was fairly complete, and probably he had only slight interest in it. His unique contribution to American historiography was the theory that the British lost the American War of Independence because they failed to hire enough Hessians to fight for them.

He was a large and gruffly pleasant fellow with a shiny dome and an aroma of stale cigar smoke marking him in his travels through the building. He encouraged his thirteen-year-old scholars to call him "Moose," a practice which even his most progressive colleagues thought regret-
hand out his assignments and then amble over to the desk tably lacking in dignity. Moose did not care. He liked to of one of his sports-minded students. He would sit down on top of the desk and signal for three or four like-minded boys to gather around. At this point a lively seminar would commence on the Detroit Tigers baseball game of the previous evening. Meanwhile the rest of the class would break up into small groups, which combined to produce a tremendous noise inside the classroom. Some girl might shout for silence, but Moose would order the protesting girl to shut up before he mildly reproved everyone else. After five minutes the noise would return to its previous level, Moose contributing in no small part with his heated denunciations of the current Tiger manager.

But occasionally Moose would hear the call of duty. Rising from our baseball seminar, he would touch the first two fingers of his right hand to his teeth, and issue a powerful whistle. Few students would take this seriously, and so next Moose would have to roar, "Hey, shut up back there, will ya?" But there were invariably a few fellows who refused to believe that Moose was serious about having a quiet classroom, and simply ignored him. So Moose would lift up an eraser from the blackboard, fix his aim on one of the last rioters, and let the thing fly. While the stunned lad shook off this blow, Moose would shout at him, "O'Leary, you bum, I told you to keep your mouth shut!" After that we would carry on in silence, each of us as startled by the turn of events as poor O'Leary. Such episodes were rare in our suburban school, and Moose could get away with his part in them only because he was otherwise so amiable.

Similarly, the innocent incompetence of the athletic director at the great suburban public high school I attended was for a long time tolerated as causing no irreparable harm to school life. He was a man known (although never to his face) as Big Ed. In fact, he was big nowhere but in his belly. Little more than five feet tall, he was shaped like a potato, with a trim crew cut topping him off. Although a native of these States, Ed's command of the language was unsteady. This put him well within the great tradition of American athletic directors, but even so his difficulties were unique. His mind seemed always to be playing nasty tricks on his tongue. Most startling was his addiction to the phrase "off of it" in the place where other people employ "y'know." A Big Ed sentence would go something like this: "Youse guys haven't won three games all year, off of it!" Sometimes he would repeat this "off of it" two or three times consecutively, as if he were an imbecile. One day three or four of us gathered around him and started a conversation. After a minute or so, we found ourselves dismayed that he was speaking in an unusually intelligible manner. So one member of our group was inspired to introduce an "off of it" of his own into the discussion. The ruse was successful: Big Ed babbled away, the "off of its" came faster than we could count them, and the chat was afterward judged a success.

It was Big Ed's misfortune as athletic director to find himself caught up in a small way with the angry political atmosphere of the times. This was during the Vietnam years, and the minority of students who took any interest in politics were indignantly opposed to the war. Big Ed, in contrast, had once been heard to say, "I voted for Wallace, off of it," and word of this got around. It actually offended few people, serving mainly to bolster self-confidence by offering clear evidence of Big Ed's deep inferiority to everyone around him.

But at last there arrived an occasion when Ed's sensibilities became a matter of schoolwide interest. I played no small part in this, as at the time I had editorial responsibility for the school newspaper and was itching for controversies. One day a letter to the editor arrived in the newspaper office, signed by a member of the school tennis team, which complained that the writer had been ordered to cut his hair before he would be allowed to compete. I was confronted with a deadline only one day away, and the letter seemed to me as much an epistle of salvation as if it had been written by Paul of Tarsus himself. Despite my best efforts to conjure up some feverish apparition, it appeared that my front page was likely to give news of the senior prom and similarly dreadful and respectable stuff. Now I saw a way out. I dashed over to the mock-up and slashed the front page apart. I dispatched one reporter to find the tennis player, and ordered another to hunt down Big

Ed. My plan was to run two stories side by side, the tennis player denouncing, and Big Ed defending, the measure. I tossed away the column I had scheduled for the issue, and quickly banged out another, denouncing coaches and supportive athletes as agents of dark forces. The era of dress codes in public schools was coming to an end, and so the present incident came as something of a surprise and was sure to arouse interest.

Soon the reporters returned with their stories. The tennis player offered predictable and sensible complaints against the restrictive policy, but Big Ed's rebuttal was more than I could have hoped for. It included about a dozen "off of its," which I deleted, fearing trouble with the school administration. For similar reasons I revised his syntax. Even after all that, the substance of his argument remained remarkable. He argued that coaches must have unquestioned authority over the lives of their athletes, suggesting that this ought often to exceed the authority of parents. This power in his view derived justly from the superior wisdom of coaches. For instance, they *knew* that if athletes were not forced to cut their hair, they would perspire unnecessarily, potentially causing defeat. Long hair was likely to fall over the athlete's eyes, causing injury to result from temporary blindness in the midst of competition. Big Ed also felt that the use of headbands was a case of treating the symptoms rather than the disease. The fact that professional tennis players used them was, in his view, quite irrelevant to the situation of the high school athlete. The opinion of any coach was infallible.

The publication of these views caused an uproar. The minority who agreed with the hair-cutting policy thought Ed's explanation of it ludicrous, while everyone else denounced "the fascist," employing the term in the contemporary, light-hearted manner. Even the coaches were embarrassed. Students snickered whenever they passed the athletic director's office.

I felt sorry for Big Ed. Fortunately he was oblivious to the storm raging around him, as no one said anything to his face. Oddly enough, it was the tennis player who rescued him from this abuse. He announced that he did not wish to make a great issue of his protest, that he mainly wanted to play tennis, and therefore would cut his hair. Although his comments had no immediate effect on his career, Big Ed seemed never to recover from the wide exposure of his mind. Thereafter other teachers abandoned their usual collegial rectitude and denounced him in front of students. Coaches started demanding, and getting, more control over their own budgets. After another couple of years (by which time I had graduated and was only checking back to see how matters had proceeded without me), it seemed that Big Ed had been stripped of all responsibility. I found him sitting in his office one day, reading freshman football schedules. I thought I would needle him a bit, as he was usually a good-humored fellow. I said I was happy to see that he had through his scheduling assured the school of another losing team. "Oh, no, I didn't," he responded, grinning. "The coach took care of this. I'm out of this, off of it." He did not seem unhappy; after all he was tenured and collecting his full salary. But he was a man very much out of place. It may be too hard on our ancestors to say that he was also out of his era. Like Moose, he would have fit in better among the faculty of my old school in Detroit. When their schoolteaching careers had begun in the suburbs, these men had surely been more typical of their order. But as the years passed and the suburbs grew, the younger teachers started to move in. They were wilier than the old guard, more carefully trained in the art of concealing the tyranny of the teacher. The professors of education had instilled the spirit of cooperation in them, and convinced them they were agents of democracy. This meant that the immediate needs and desires of students ought always to be remembered.

To the student, this meant it was more likely one would be beaten over the head with a feather than with a yardstick. The nature of amusing incidents changed. I recall a young teacher of tenth-grade English, who had announced a course of instruction in lyric verse. A record player was at her side, with a record of Simon and Garfunkel tunes spinning around on it. She placed the needle in its groove, and listened with her thirty students to a song which had been heard at least twenty-five times by anyone who had listened to a radio in the past two weeks. When the song was finished she lifted the needle and looked the class over. "That's my idea of poetry," she said. "What's yours?" Silence was followed by a collective mumble. A girl with frizzy hair raised her hand and offered the opinion that Leonard Cohen must be counted among the greatest poets of all time. The teacher said this was "interesting," and called on a tall, thin boy who differed with the girl and thought that Bob Dylan was the first among poets of the twentieth century; his words and music were profounder than anyone else's. He started to recite some of Dylan's lyrics, and another boy started to sing one of his songs.

"*Very* interesting," said the teacher, interrupting. She asked for other examples of great poetry. A lad at the back of the room mentioned John Donne.

After brief silence, the teacher looked him over and said, "Yes, of course—in a more old-fashioned vein."

Another boy cried out, "John Donne doesn't mean a [pause while he checks himself] thing to anybody anymore!"

The teacher thought about this for a moment and then

said, "Well, we're all entitled to our opinions. That's what criticism is all about!" The subject was pretty much exhausted, and within a few minutes the conversation ended and an open reading session began.

Allowing for the interchangeability of bards, it may be assumed that similar sessions are going on today, as this teacher is still in business. So is another English teacher, an amiable fellow with twenty years of classroom dust in his nostrils. He was always fond of Shakespeare, but two days into *King Lear,* he found his sixteen-year-olds looking bewildered and more than slightly bored. Maybe two or three among the thirty in class seemed genuinely interested in the old man's roaring at cataracts and hurricanoes. The teacher scratched his graying curls and shuffled his Hush Puppies. Suddenly he announced, "You know, there's some question about whether Shakespeare really wrote these plays. In fact, there's a great deal of doubt about the identity of Shakespeare." One head lifted itself from a cradle of arms on a desk. A pair of eyes opened up in the third row. And so the teacher dragged out the various theories of Shakespearean authorship, and the reading of *King Lear* was set aside.

Over in the social studies wing, there was a teacher of government who decided that it was boring to speak of the separation of powers and tedious to waste his eloquence and the students' ears on explications of the pocket veto. So he proposed, in the most benevolent but assured manner he could muster, that the class spend its next month participating in a "mock United Nations session." His proposal cleared its first hurdle. Nobody commented that a mock United Nations session was a redundancy. Everyone appeared to accept the idea as one worthy of a class in government. Provision was made for the teacher to perform simultaneously as Kurt Waldheim and General Assembly president, thus giving him complete control over events. One-quarter of the class was Jewish, and so there was heavy competition to play the part of the noble, beleaguered delegate of the state of Israel. The teacher suggested that someone represent South Africa, as at the time the South Africans had not been booted out of the United Nations; perhaps this class would undertake the job. A rather bright, fat boy agreed to the assignment. Before long each student had accepted a nation for his representation; because there were only thirty-or-so students, several African and Latin American republics went unrepresented. The teacher set out an agenda and some of the students engaged in research, but most of them borrowed from the researches of four or five well-read classmates, and this pleasant fantasy was played out for a month.

Also in the social studies department, there was a teacher of an elite course in Russian history. Often he suspended his disquisitions on the boyhood of the last Tsar Nicholas and the fate of the battleship *Potemkin*. His students were used to this. On various occasions, he had detoured from Russian history into discussions of the *Whole Earth Catalogue*, the philosophy of Lao-tse, and the Fourteen Points of Woodrow Wilson. Each time his lectures had been based upon his desultory reading of the previous evening. Now, once again, the Russian history teacher was feeling particularly inspired. He had attended his master's class in education the previous evening, and listened to the instructor exhort the teachers to "gauge the sensibility of the class anew each day and penetrate its consciousness with carefully nuanced realities." Afterward he had gone to see a performance of the Marx Brothers' *Animal Crackers* for the sixth time. He decided to discuss the Marx Brothers with his Russian history students. When he raised the subject he discerned that approximately half the class had seen a Marx Brothers movie at some time or other, another fourth had heard good things about the Marx Brothers, and only one-fourth seemed completely uninterested. He decided to continue, figuring that educational democracy was the loser if he stopped. At the end of the hour he was satisfied with himself. The class, on the whole, was happy enough to avoid hearing about doomed monarchs and hirsute revolutionaries for another day.

Downstairs in the foreign language department, a bosomy Spanish teacher fast approaching the end of her blossom time was performing one of the rites of foreign language-teaching: the memoir of the youthful trip to Spain. This was a delicious moment squeezed into an awful routine of verb conjugations, readings of infantile poetry, and sessions with the subjunctive. The Spanish teacher was unmarried. She knew that in the next room one of her colleagues, a stout lady with twenty-five years of wedded bliss and dinners soaked with olive oil behind her, was giving her version of the Spanish journey, and was recalling the hour when the daylight faded from the old quarter of Granada, and she and her friends found themselves stranded on a tiny street, uncertain of where to turn—when suddenly they heard a serenade, offered by two young men on a nearby balcony, who invited them up for a pitcher of sangria, and were politely rejected, the girls having suddenly discovered the right way out to the boulevard. As a younger woman, this Spanish teacher did not wish to tell it like that. So she said she was in Seville, not Granada, and she added knowingly that Seville was the lovelier and more romantic of the two cities. She was alone; her two friends had gone off by themselves. She heard the serenade, was invited up for sangria—and accepted. And after that? "It was, well, you know, a nice time: one I'll always remember"—after which she returned to *el vocabulario*.

My flight into the airy realms of higher education was very brief, but I had time enough to tune in on dull professors and brilliant ones. At the university, knowledge enforced by eloquence will serve a professor well; there is little fussing over educational techniques, as on the lower levels. Nevertheless, pedagogical talent was neither more nor less common in the professoriat than among common schoolteachers. Learning merely grows more specialized, and so those who have mastered some area of the arts or sciences assume that they need not work too hard to communicate it. Students reflect their boredom in different ways. I merely excused myself from the proceedings, having grown impatient of receiving the wisdom of paid instructors. I calculated that if these distinguished ladies and gentlemen had anything worth saying, they would say them in their books, which I could purchase and peruse at my leisure. And so I retired from education, and began to live.

Whatever their tactical defects, the old-fashioned disciplinarians were certainly the most memorable in their deficiencies. I hope a few of them stay active for a while, so that the next generation can see what a lively and hilarious affair education can be. In my time I was educated by more than one hundred teachers. I believe that I remember them all, but only because I am cursed with a good memory. My friends assure me that most of them were utterly forgettable, and when I call up the name of this or that chalky wretch, I am likely to be met with blank faces. This is especially true of the hermetic instructors in mathematics or the sciences. There were, of course, exceptions. After consuming two bottles of champagne I can be led to believe that 5 per cent of my teachers were first-rate, and another 10 per cent put forth an honest and conscientious effort which yielded results. But I will go no further than that. There is a great deal of gaseous sentimentality regarding schoolteachers, due mainly to the fact that they get hold of us at an early age and a sentimental haze overwhelms our thoughts when we try to recall them.

Nevertheless, I am bound to wonder what makes a good teacher and why most teachers are so bad. The answer to the first question, it seems to me, is as obvious as it is impossible to state in categorical terms. The good teacher has a genuine interest in his subject, and a natural gift for communication; the interest outweighs the likely limitation of his knowledge, and the gift for communication is something innate and unteachable. The only teachers worthy of the title are quite immune to theories of their art, even as the only writers worth reading are quite immune to the prescriptions of a Lionel Trilling or F. R. Leavis. What, in this scheme, is the role of the school of education? Almost certainly, its function is to mitigate the answer to my second question. Most teachers are bad quite simply because they lack the innate talent which makes teachers good. The school of education exists in order to deny this obvious fact and pad the denial with a multitude of unintelligible theories about the nature of education. Once it is understood that schools are no more the natural places for children and youths than fishbowls are the natural places for fish, the problem becomes more comprehensible. The educator feels compelled to justify or at least explain the compromise that is involved.

Civilization is filled with such compromises and such explanations. Thus a police officer in any American city does not admit that he is a police officer because he enjoys swaggering before the public and bashing an occasional head; he professes that he is a lover of law, order, and the Constitution of the United States. Thus the average newspaper reporter is reluctant to confess that the thrill of his work is in seeing the head of a public official swim, or in uncovering some swindle which will alarm his readers and make them lose their appetite for dinner; he says that he is a lover of truth who reveres the First Amendment. And thus the educator announces that there is science as well as art in his task, and that the quality of teaching can somehow be quantified.

Do I counsel, in these circumstances, either a reversion to the hickory switch or more of the soothing modern methods? It should be plain that I am quite impartial in such disputes, that the whole debate seems to me of the slightest interest. It is little more than a rivalry between different forms of bad teaching. After all, the business of schooling is little more than a matter of simple domestication and minimal enlightenment; individual initiative takes care of the rest. The educators would of course have us believe that the reverse is true, and that institutions make the man. If you agree with them, proceed directly to the next chapter.

Allowing that the first-rate teacher will manage to assert himself and that there is nothing to be done about the rest of them, I am left high and dry in my search for reforms. I can do no more than suggest that the idiotic idealism which surrounds all discussion of education be abandoned. This is as likely an occurrence as all American patriots rising up in unison to denounce Abraham Lincoln. Yet it would be a happy event. Parents would view their own responsibilities more seriously, and educators would cease to be more respectable figures than garage mechanics or shoe salesmen. As things stand today, educators will continue to prattle that they are uplifting humanity and enriching democracy, parents will continue to think it important whether their children enter one suburban school system rather than another, and the janissaries of Maria Montessori will continue to evoke raised eyebrows. All this is a pity.

A Tourist Among Faiths

I am a tourist among faiths, a wanderer among certainties in a land where religion's righteousness is valued above its poetry. A Frenchman or Italian works up an enthusiasm for churchgoing by contemplating the musty aroma and grand acoustics of his hometown cathedral. The German or English Protestant is a participant in robust harmonies, and is persuaded by the music of Bach that somewhere in Heaven sits a God whose ears are perked for the sound of a chorale. There are of course similar Americans, but they have never composed the majority. Think of the creeds that have sprouted from the soil of the New World: Unitarianism, which is less a faith than an intellectual exercise; Christian Science, a preposterous heresy invoking literacy in the name of faith; or southern Baptism, which survives in varied forms as a celebration of ignorance. I can no more picture a quattrocento Florentine comprehending these than I can picture a county sewage commissioner from suburban Milwaukee beaming his delight at a canvas of Fra Angelico. Perhaps even more instructive are the priestly reform movements which have cracked the older religious orders and established themselves comfortably in America, bringing us Jews who do not know the kosher laws apart from a current dietary craze, and bringing lady priests into the stuffy chapels of Episcopalia. A sort of spontaneous Protestantism has established itself as the dominant factor in national religious life. The country that brought you the Unitarians, the Shakers and the Mormons has now unveiled the right-to-lifer, the super-Zionist, the quasi-Buddhist and all the others who have kept the air buzzing in recent years. It is a bewildering spectacle, and many of us find ourselves in the position of the Frenchman of an earlier generation who informed an American friend of his intention to leave the Catholic Church, and was asked in turn what sort of Protestantism he intended to take up. "I have lost my faith," the Frenchman responded, "but not my reason."

I.   THE CONFUSION
OF THE CATHOLICS

Although I am myself too young to remember them, I sometimes come across accounts of Archbishop Sheen's televised lectures in the 1950s. In my mind's eye I see him standing there, a piece of chalk in hand and a blackboard at his rear, hammering home the ABCs of faith. It is a picture too disturbing for my mind to absorb, and so I hasten to chase it away. In later years this gentleman conducted his televised Easter sunrise services from the Hollywood Bowl. Once upon an Easter morning I found myself in front of the tube, confronting that thatch of stiff white hair

and those rolling blue eyes. I do not recall why I was so engaged at that hour of the morning. As a non-Christian I
was without spiritual obligations and free to indulge my
habit of late sleeping; instead I was watching an archbishop
wave his arms on television. There was a dreamy quality to
this proceeding, and it soon lulled me back to sleep, during
which my mind went to work on Sheen and transformed
him into a schoolmaster of the old-fashioned sort, an asso-
ciate of the yardstick wavers and eraser throwers of my
early youth. Before his image retired from my dreams, he
had harangued me with his views on Christ and had
dispatched me to a corner of the classroom where I was expected to master his precepts. I have since, in turning my
television dial, met up with the archbishop two or three
times, but I have never stopped to linger with him. It is not
that my dream has haunted me, but rather that the concerns of this holy character seemed so totally unrelated to
my own that to spend time with him was to waste it.

I am told that younger American Catholics today have
little more than a nodding acquaintance with this once-
eminent archbishop, and that the televised Easter services
no more displayed his hold on the national imagination
than Joe DiMaggio's advertisements for a coffee-making
machine reflect the glory of that faded magnifico of the dia-
mond. This is not surprising. American Catholicism has become such a dreary affair that even a skeptic is saddened
by it. Even at its worst, the Church of Rome affected glorious colors and a mysterious dignity. Its subscribers were in
some way distinctive, and recognizable to the rest of us.
Entering a Catholic church and listening to the Latin lit-.
urgy was a vaguely threatening affair; one sensed a challenge to one's own way of life. The Catholicism of one's
school friends seemed a serious business, and we were
taught to respect it. The best pitcher on the Little League

team wore his St. Christopher's medal, and sometimes attributed his success to it. The public schools offered their respects by serving fish for lunch on Fridays. Catholics were incontestably different, which in turn made their Catholicism interesting. I imagine that this has not changed completely, but the mystique of Catholicism has been heavily diluted. With the endless varieties of horrid food served in school lunchrooms, it would now seem very odd to receive fish sticks every Friday. I suppose that St. Christopher's medals are still worn, but any Little League pitcher who attributed his success to this medal would be thought obscure or at least puzzling by his non-Catholic teammates. A visit to a Catholic church no longer means a confrontation with the ancient Latin; instead one hears a language which is worse than plain English, in that it intends to convey soaring sentiments in the flat intonations of trade. I have witnessed recent Christmas midnight masses, and have found them sorry spectacles. Cardinals, as well-oiled and perfumed as their predecessors, have appeared near to falling asleep at the sound of their own voices. Their proclamations of wonder at the magnificence of their faith sound so perfunctory as to seem preposterous. They are reduced to the level of Methodist country parsons, with the reminder of a glorious past inflicting keener pains than any Methodist has ever known.

The decline of American Catholicism has been astonishingly rapid; less than two decades ago the face of Pope John XXIII beamed from the covers of the national magazines; there was general agreement that the Pope was a superior fellow—a kind of Rotarian with unusual spiritual gifts—and that the Church he led might be regarded as a legitimate agency of human enlightenment. What the Pope failed to accomplish in spreading goodwill toward Catholics, the Kennedy presidency handled. Even after the

Kennedy assassination, the superb performances of his family—especially the women in it—inspired in many people the notion that Catholicism was more successful than other faiths in providing spiritual fortification for troubled humanity. After a long history of American anti-Catholicism, there was at last evidence that the Catholic Church was one of those ideas whose time had come. Many intellectuals, their careers sustained by such notions, found this idea especially thrilling.

A conspiracy of events brought these proceedings to a prompt and seedy end. The trouble started when the civil rights movement showed signs of getting out of hand. Catholics of varied political leanings had previously benefited from the cultural insularity provided by their one true Church. Even the Coughlin pestilence of the thirties involved no great introspection among Catholics; Father C.'s sly Jew-baiting may have slightly discomfited the more civilized American Catholics, but no substantial moral issue was involved. His superiors finally shut him up because he became a political liability, not because he threatened the souls of his parishioners. In contrast, the Negro revolution provoked much soul-searching among all the religions, and when finally it involved such things as the busing of black schoolchildren into the Irish Catholic precincts of South Boston, it touched off a minor convulsion. American Catholics might have settled amicably enough with the Negroes, except they were hardly the only matter with which men of true morality were required to deal. The Vietnam war provided another distraction from pure faith. It was hard to determine whether God's will was best served by slaughtering yellow men on behalf of the national honor, or by staying home and quoting Jesus Christ on the subject of peace to the local draft board. Both the civil rights movement and the Vietnam war were episodes which affected all

Americans but were especially unsettling to those among them interested in executing God's will. Even more damaging was the startling preoccupation of the Catholic Church with sexual matters. It was the Church's misfortune to assume views which any twelve-year-old, freshly aware of the peculiar powers forming in his scrotum, would find laughable. Even worse, the lad's grandfather, after doing his duty with a gentle reprimand, would ease himself into a soft chair and laugh twice as hard. Now a modern Pope, working beneath the searchlights of modern publicists and without armies at his command, is subjected to constraints that would have made some of his lusty and powerful predecessors forsake ambition for the job. But a fair supply of political shrewdness will assist him in his ascent to the top of the Church, and it might be hoped that he will know when to refrain from enforcing his views as a matter of doctrine. Unfortunately for the Catholic Church, things did not always work out this way with Pope Paul VI, and so there was almost as much denial of the obvious in *Humanae Vitae* and succeding pronouncements as in the collected state papers of the Hon. Dean Rusk. Here we find the argument that the use of contraceptives will ultimately destroy a man's respect for his wife by encouraging his engagement in too frequent intercourse with her; in other words, according to the late Paul, correct sexual rhythm is the foundation upon which sound marriages are built.* Here, too, we find the Pope running on about reason and free will, and implying their derivation from sexual abstinence within marriage. Here, also, is the argument that parents who refrain from contraceptives will do a more splendid job of raising their children than parents who employ them; as the Pope put it, "Parents acquire the

---

* Much of this was carried forward from the *Casti connubii* of Pius XI. John Paul II also finds this point of view agreeable.

capacity of having a deeper and more efficacious influence on the education of their offspring; little children and youths grow up with a just appraisal of human values, and in the serene and harmonious development of their spiritual and sensitive faculties." So it seems that this Pope maintained distinctive views of married life—but perhaps Paul, whose cultivation was widely celebrated, lulled himself to sleep nights by listening to the Goldberg Variations, and was thus sublimely unaware of the itches that afflict much of humanity at nightfall. Anyway there is little doubt that the papal encyclicals, however warmly received in rural Ecuador, were on the whole an embarrassment to American Catholics. They made the Church appear hopelessly out of step with the world, and being out of step is the contemporary American version of original sin.

So the public image of Catholicism dissolved into mud, and was left in the hands of free slingers. The old moderates, ranging from Archbishop Sheen to the boys camped out in the secular city, faded into dull memories, and in their place arose angry men and women from the flanks, hollering about war, social injustice, contraceptives and abortion. The Berrigans held the stage for an hour in the late sixties, speaking with the dazzling dim-wittedness of prophets and cheered on by the likes of Garry Wills: "It is time to join the underground." But after a while they chose marriage and bitterness over activism and hysteria, and retired from the scene. When the dust cleared on the Left, only a few spokesmen remained to urge the mightiest and most indignant causes through respectable channels. Where Sheen had invaded the national mind a decade earlier, his place had been taken by the likes of Father Robert Drinan, Doctor of Laws and spiritual descendent of Ignatius Loyola. Drinan's fire-breathing became nationally known in 1970, when he ran successfully for Congress in the Fifth District of Massachusetts. Around that time he issued a book called *Vietnam and Armageddon: Peace, War, and the Christian Conscience,* in which his distinctive method of moral-political discourse became evident in such lines as this: "If one accepts the stark fact that the United States can contribute to peace only by some courageous, unilateral method of slowing down the arms race then it follows that the Catholics of America are involved in a collective silence which makes the silence of German Catholics in the decade of Hitler's atrocities seem almost insignificant by contrast." Here, as in the papal encyclicals, we find the unbending generalizations, the air of single-minded righteousness, the belief that a single action (or restraint) can reverse the historical tide, and the fundamental craziness of the whole proposal. The padre is, after all, suggesting that if only we lay down enough of our arms, the Russians will be inspired to do the same, and that furthermore this American initiative would be "courageous" rather than idiotic.

Several years after the publication of this treatise and its author's election to the House of Representatives, I was awakened from my political slumber in the tranquil state of Michigan by the alarming news that a family friend was undertaking a challenge of the godly congressman. I was invited to assist in the enterprise, but without promise of remuneration. Therefore I required repeated assurances that Drinan was indeed still regarded as one of the moral heroes of our time and that I would consequently be cast in the heretical role with which I am most comfortable. Eventually I went aboard and spent an amusing month with the campaign. Most of my time was spent in acts of verbal incineration of the Drinan record. These took the form of speech drafts which were usually set aside by the candidate on the assigned dates of delivery. I was consoled by explanations that my words were too eloquent for the audience of ignoramuses he was scheduled to address. Once in a while I would bang out a press release (although this was not my main job) which would "deplore" a statement of Drinan's or register "shock" at learning of some unfortunate vote the congressman had made in subcommittee three years earlier. Once or twice I had the thrill of seeing these releases quoted in the newspaper of a decaying factory town in central Massachusetts. Otherwise I am afraid my actual contributions to the campaign were very slight; it is possible that I was on balance a negative influence.

My wholehearted support of my friend's effort to attain the job of his dreams was, I believe, uncorrupted by any thought that his office-seeking could be equated with a crusade. It is regrettable, and no doubt due to their being underpaid, that campaign workers habitually employ the metaphors of crusade in order to justify their own labors. Most candidates know better, and except in their public pronouncements they tend to avoid this sort of delusion— at least my friend did. My own perverse nature often prompted me to remind my colleagues at campaign headquarters that we were basically involved in little more than an effort to help a decent fellow unseat a Christian cad. I thought then, and still think, that this was an admirable objective, but it seemed an unsatisfactory explanation to my colleagues, and even an irritation. Although I remained on cordial terms with them, and was indeed given the special consideration due to an unemployed scribe from the lands beyond the Berkshires, I was obviously regarded with some suspicion. The campaign manager, a young and attractive woman who smoked her cigarettes fiercely and tolerated sycophants more gladly than skeptics, managed eventually to squeeze me out of any active participation in the campaign, although toward the end she suggested that I might

succeed brilliantly at the distribution of leaflets in local
shopping centers. She was probably more grateful than I
was when, after I had been in Massachusetts for a month, I
was lured away by the sudden development of other business. At the time a month remained before the voting, and
in my absence Drinan carried off the election. The margin
was very narrow, and election analysts failed to take account of the effect of my absence on the result.

Anyway, I had only one occasion during my brief career as an activist to confront the holy congressman. It was
a singularly inauspicious event—a small fair in an uninteresting mid-Massachusetts town (the name of which I
have forgotten), conducted on a lovely September afternoon. A couple dozen wiry New Englanders wandered
around the village green, munching on sticky buns, sipping
very sweet cider, and waiting to hear the two congressional
candidates' prescriptions for salvation. Our man went first,
delivering what was in truth a rather dull little speech, and
following it up with a few respectable answers to some
childish questions from his customers. Afterward he
strolled around the green, shaking hands, until at last he
started to look bewildered and was shipped off to his next
campaign stop. Drinan had been scheduled to follow our
man's speech with one of his own, but after a half hour he
was nowhere in sight. Our campaign manager explained
that this was a shrewd ploy on Drinan's part. His own pre-
sentation was so likely to appear second-rate after our
man's performance, she said, that he wanted to delay it as
long as possible, in order to make comparison difficult.
At last Drinan arrived, and apologized to the folks for his
chauffeur having made a wrong turn. Our campaign manager muttered a few words which included "liar" but which
were not widely heard, and the congressman lurched into a
conventional denunciation of the rich sinners who threat-

ened to dismantle the welfare state he had been so instru-
mental in constructing. There was applause, after which
Drinan joined his constituents in washing down the speech
with cider. Then he started on a handshaking tour, a thin,
nervous figure enclosed by his collar, his priestly garb covered by a frayed black blazer which was flecked with white
droppings from his bald scalp. I looked forward to meeting
him, and concentrated my thoughts on an impertinent utterance, but as he approached I decided that as a loyal
campaign worker I had best restrain my impulse and speak
respectfully. And so at last I inhaled his foul breath, took
his damp hand into mine, and exchanged polite greetings.
Then, just as he seemed prepared to say something else,
Drinan's tense face opened into a broad and astonishing
grin, his hand dropped, and he dashed suddenly to a spot
ten feet behind me where a young mother was burping her
baby. He commented approvingly on her work, and then
posed with mother and baby in front of a local photog-
rapher's camera. It was as if Ignatius Loyola had suddenly
been recomposed in the image of Hubert Humphrey.

As I have indicated, my career as a political apparat-
chik ended shortly thereafter, although my informers regularly brought me up to date on the exchange of scurrilities.
After his return to Congress, Drinan published another
book, this time arguing that our unilateral reduction of
arms should by no means preclude steady shipments of
weaponry to Israel; the numerous Jews in Drinan's district
found this a heartening message. In early 1978 the congressman, as so often in the past, rose in the House to offer
some Christian support for a liberal cause, in this case the
feminist movement. The period allowed for ratification of
the Equal Rights Amendment should be extended, he argued, not for any political or constitutional reason, but for
a moral one. The proponents of the amendment could not

possibly have foreseen the "national campaign of extortion" which would be waged against it. No evidence was offered. A charitable gentleman! A great Christian leader! A model of Holy Roman conduct in earthly affairs!

Drinan's emergence—and that of less well-known seminarians with similar views and perhaps better manners—should be regarded as a political rather than a religious development. It is quite possible that his demagoguery would have been just as successful if he had never worn the collar; indeed, in his congressional district he found himself greatly belabored by his fellow Catholics, and rarely bothered to go begging for their support. But his tone is typical of the contemporary Catholic commenting on public matters; the shrill indignation is the characteristic thing. One need only slide over the political spectrum to see this. What is it that exercises the minds of more traditional Catholics? Not the disappearance of the Latin liturgy, for this is a question of aesthetics not easily treated in a republic which disdains the combination of religious belief and sound taste. Not some issue of technical theology, as the contemporary American of whatever faith is relatively unconcerned with whether or not his religion is rational; he trusts that the matter is not fundamentally important. Instead, the Catholic mind busies itself with the unpleasant question of whether or not American women should be permitted to abort the births of unwanted children. Our habit of thinking of public issues in terms of left-wing and right-wing perspective obscures the fact that the voice of a Drinan and that of a right-to-lifer harmonize well in the American chorus. It was entirely suitable that the abortion controversy followed the Vietnam war on the roster of moral issues. After one faction ceased ordering Presidents of the United States to say how many babies they had recently burned, another faction arose with its photographs of bloody fetuses, and similarly demanded to know how a civilized society could countenance such murder. Both groups employed the traditional techniques of American rabble-rousing, which involve getting hold of issues which are easily inflamed by angry rhetoric, and then performing upon them without mercy until an indifferent public is compelled to regard them as great moral issues. So if you happen to favor more military spending or oppose the Equal Rights Amendment you are in the eyes of Drinan a coward or an extortionist. If you are inclined to tolerate abortions as often making the best of bad situations, you are a murderer in the eyes of the right-to-lifer. Under these circumstances, it is practically impossible to discuss any moral question in the United States of America; the curse of democracy is too much with us. And so the American Catholic with any sense of honor is likely to function as a secret Protestant, finding, if he is lucky, a sympathetic priest, and otherwise conducting his otherworldly affairs in the privacy of his own soul. He has no more sense of affiliation with his fellow Catholics than he has with the aspirations of a Mennonite missionary wandering through the African jungle. He is hounded by the caddish invocations of morality by his brothers and sisters in Christ; he is rebuked by a Pope who issues foolish encyclicals; he is bewildered by a republic which daily finds new reasons to disdain his ancient and honorable faith; and so he retires to worship his God in private, praying that he will be left alone.

II. THE ALTAR OF ZION

For perhaps the first time in history, the Jews have it better. Indeed, the situation of the contemporary American Jew is so pleasant that it is a wonder we have not yet seen massive conversions to the Mosaic creed. I myself enjoyed the advantage of being raised as a Jew during the past quarter-century, and were my spirit willing I would regularly join the friends of my youth in their proclamations of faith. Unfortunately my constitution does not permit this, and I am frequently reduced to the sort of bilious nay-saying which leaves half my friends suspecting my Jewishness, and the other half begging me to travel to the Holy Land, in order that my faith might undergo the purification process which presumably overtakes you there.

My friends are quite right to suspect my faith, for I have none worth talking about, although I do enjoy a pretty sermon and will wait longer than most men to hear a cantor land upon a clear note. But for several years I have known that the concerns of contemporary Jews do not pertain so much to religion as to a more general mythology, and it is this which I shall consider here.

Although the Jews are famous for their devotion to learning, their reputations in this regard derive from the hoary days when they floundered around the ghettos of Europe, and the authorities restricted their enterprises. Scholarship, especially of the biblical and talmudic sort, was in such circumstances a happy alternative to the sinful recreations of the goyim. More recently, when Jews have been able to pursue whatever happened to interest them, the interest in scholarship has instead become more of an interest in useful education, and so Jews have found their way into law, medicine and the other noble and remunerative professions. Many of them have, upon entering these professions, retained the ancient belief that they are carrying on as members of a race of scholars, but this is akin to my walking the sidewalks of New York shoeless, smoking a corncob pipe, and announcing that I am carrying on the tradition of Huckleberry Finn. With individual exceptions, the contemporary Jew is not scholarly at all, and so he has his sense of Jewish history compressed into a few searing myths which form themselves into a useful sequence. He is familiar enough with the Bible to suspect he belongs to a great and even superior tradition. He might even be able to recite the Ten Commandments by heart, although this is not likely, and the 24th Psalm will certainly stump him. He knows that after the biblical period the Jews were dispersed rather friendlessly into the world, and that the creation of the diaspora resulted in two millennia of persecution and horror. Although this meant exposure to such events as the Spanish Inquisition, the primary experience in the memory of the American Jew is Eastern European. It was from the Slavic lands that most of them escaped to America and began their climb to prosperity and social respectability. When Hitler started his slaughter, American Jews were still haunted by their memories of the nights on which muzhiks had chased them through the countryside. Interest in Palestine among American Jews was at this time slight, and many regarded the Zionists among them as a hotheaded and unpalatable bunch. Even after World War II, when the creation of the Israeli state was still in doubt, support for the idea among American Jews was by no means unanimous.

All that changed with the establishment of Israel and the ensuing struggle of that state to stay in business. By the 1950s a new generation was coming of age in America which had known not Russia. Subsequently another generation (my own) would arise which had not known Hitler either. Gradually, history was supplanted by mythology in the American Jewish mind. Such a development was inevitable. By the 1960s the survivors of muzhik clubbings were grandparents; chances are that moderate prosperity had enabled them to enter into old age with their memories of youth somewhat softened, and so if they bothered to tell their grandchildren anything of the old days, and the grandchildren bothered to listen (as native Americans it is possible they adopted the national aversion to history), the stories would most likely retain the juicier moments and leave out the dull parts. Similarly younger Jews would get their image of the Hitler era by listening to Daddy's attractively embellished war stories, by viewing old movies, and by reading indignant books. They would watch with comfortable anguish as the Russian brethren carried on the old-fashioned struggle against persecution, no doubt remaining aware that it is practically impossible for someone pleasantly situated to share the emotions of his brother in hell.

Throughout these years the American Jew has desired some focus for his faith, and in such circumstances the utility of Jehovah has been limited. The Lord God of the Torah is, after all, a mighty unpleasant character; indeed, he is a kind of enormous scoundrel, unreasonable and threatening, with thunderbolts always at his side. He was a good God for a frightened people, for he served to remind them that their course in life, however miserable, was righteous, and that their uneasily attained virtue stood to be rewarded. The poor Jew in his ghetto, nibbling at his kosher meat and mumbling his prayers, was able to find spiritual sustenance in this gloomy testament. But a man one or two generations removed from the authority of tsars and Polish policemen, who has been treated to American public schools and the wonderful kishka cooked up by his immigrant grandmother in her leisure hours, has no patience with such a Jehovah. He is unlikely to sit through three hours on a Saturday forenoon. He is happy enough to dunk apples in honey, and join other congregants at his synagogue for a prayerful start to the Jewish New Year. He is amenable to returning ten days later, with a solemn mask upon his face, in order to atone for his sins of the past year; quite possibly he will even fast this day. But his toleration of religious stricture is not great. His rabbi, who knows this and who knows how else to keep his customers happy, is careful in his occasional denunciations of the "twice-a-year Jews." The contemporary Jew rather likes this sort of gentle whipping, and a reminder from time to time that he is not as good a Jew as he ought to be.

This is because he, like the rest of American Jewry, has been blessed with the opportunity to redeem himself through Israel. Today's Jews are the only people around who can invest their souls in a national state, and subsequently earn applause for their moral courage. There is nothing quite like this in the known history of occidental religion, probably because there has never been a republic capable of combining luxury and optional belief like this one. And so the true convocations of the faithful today are less likely to be held in the synagogue than in the banquet hall. The highest holy day for the prosperous contemporary Jew, the day on which his faith is most fervent and his assertion of the greatness of his Jewish heritage is least vulnerable, is apt to be the day on which the local chapter of the Allied Jewish Campaign* holds its annual fund-raising dinner. It is an occasion even greater than a Bar Mitzvah, although this ceremony too has assumed lavish significance dinner. It is an occasion even greater than a Bar Mitzvah, vah, however, the problem is with the fundamental nature of the event: a boy of thirteen, his voice squeaking and his knees shaking, stands before the congregation and reads a brief passage from the Torah which has not the slightest significance for him. His achievement rests entirely upon his ability to read the passage in the original Hebrew, and

---

* Or one of the great Jewish charitable organizations.

by the time the lad gets around to the reading he is quite bored by the words and concerned only that he not stumble in his recitation of them. The reading is itself incomprehensible to all but a few members of the congregation, the size of which is increased 1,000 per cent by the fact of the Bar Mitzvah. The main event is in any case the luncheon or dinner party which takes place the same weekend. While the boy learns his lines, the parents concentrate their attention on the celebration, which customarily features indifferent cuisine, steady consumption of alcoholic beverages, and fat old aunties bestirring themselves to join nieces and nephews in awkward dancing as soon as the bandleader strikes up "Havah Nagilah"; also an unspeakable sweet table, around which all the relations gather to pick at the goodies and lament their collective lack of willpower. After this is over, guests usually return home with their love of Jewish tradition more firmly in place than it had been before the service and festivities, but, as I have indicated, the relative insignificance of the Bar Mitzvah service limits the spiritual uplift of the occasion.

No such restraints are present when the occasion is a fund-raiser for Israel. Such fund-raisers take place at several levels; there are Hadassah teas and breakfasts of the Temple Brotherhood at which contributors gather around to listen to the voice of the Prime Minister of Israel, piped in live from Jerusalem and explaining the vital importance of the funds to Jewish survival. But the campaign dinner is the greatest event of all: the big money in the community is there, the pledges issue freely from the floor, and the cause is so worthy that the contributors can easily persuade themselves that they are back in the days when merchants were princes. Mr. N., owner of a chain of hardware stores, rises to proclaim his award of $10,000 to the Israeli cause. Mr. P., the celebrated divorce lawyer, is next on the roll to be

called; he had planned to pitch in $10,0〔
now, in a sudden fit of inspiration, he anno〔
for $15,000. And the night is just starting. Dr.
loved children's dentist, declares himself for $10,
after these preliminaries, the heavy artillery is hau〔
Mr. M., the great industrialist, removes the corona fro〔
mouth, blows away a mouthful of smoke, and declares, 〔
would like to pledge $100,000 to this campaign." The
chair announces that, with this pledge, Mr. M. has exceeded last year's pledge by $20,000; in the audience a few
mumbles about monopolists are drowned out by the applause. The roll call continues: $50,000, $25,000, and on
and on; until at last Mr. N., the hardware store owner, asks
to be recognized once again, which is quickly done,
whereupon he announces that he has been so moved by tonight's show of support for Israel that he will increase his
pledge on the spot from $10,000 to $15,000. And then the
fever catches on. Dr. C., the children's dentist, reveals that
he has scratched together another $2,500 to spend in Is-
rael's name, and is now good for $12,500. And there are
other impetuously improved pledges before the evening is
out. Long before the contributors retire to their Cadillacs
and head home, the good feeling of a revival has overtaken
them; the sense of true religious fellowship has made the
evening a satisfying one. Each member of the audience has
parted with thousands of dollars on such a night, the real
figures being reduced to less awesome proportions by the
50 per cent tax rate and the charitable tax deduction now
due them; but they remain considerable. They will build
hospitals and schools in Israel, and the Prime Minister of
Israel will bless them. No crooner of the Kol Nidre will
make them feel more righteous than they do on this night.

It is no wonder that a Jew today will often make no
pretense of rationality in defending the Israeli government,

preferring instead to recall the horrors of the past, from Nasser back through Hitler to the inquisitors of Spain, and will argue, "Can't you see why it is we feel this way?" Behind all this, of course, is the sense of a liberation having occurred, of Jews at last being permitted to create a nation in their own image after millennia of diasporic anguish. Even the Jew without relatives in Israel is capable, with the barest sense of the past, of sensing the breathtaking quality of the experiment; and the goyim, too, find it a pleasure to cheer Israel on its way, regarding the Israeli government more patiently than they regard other governments, including their own. Israel has provided American Jews with what majestic purple mountains provide oafish creatures in rural Colorado: a distant object on which to focus in uncertain times. Also, it has functioned as a Montserrat to bands of unlikely Knights of the Holy Grail. The American Jew has boarded one chartered jet after another and has made his two-week pilgrimage to the Holy Land, touring the memorial, Yad Vashem, and standing at the sight of Masada, as guides inform him of his heroic past. Before he has turned for home, he will no doubt recoil from yet another plateful of kasha, and he will feel puzzled by the fuzzy malingerers at the Holy Wall, but he will nonetheless return to America with what the uplifters call a renewed sense of dedication. He will, in plainer terms, return home feeling more Jewish than when he left, and he will be proud of this.

A couple of years ago, amid researches of a trivial nature, I happened upon an issue of a bulletin regularly distributed to the members of one of the largest Reform Jewish congregations in the United States. My eyes fixed themselves upon the rabbi's column, as this rabbi was celebrated for his scholarship and eloquence. His subject on this particular occasion was "What is a Jew?" and he reported, in this connection, a recent conversation with one of his parishioners. A man had confronted him, said the rabbi, with the statement that he no longer regarded himself as a Jew. And why was that? asked the rabbi. Well, essentially, said the parishioner, although he attended services on Rosh Hashanah and Yom Kippur, he had no real belief in God, and he practiced none of the Jewish traditions. Without blinking, the rabbi said he had a question for the man: How did he feel about Israel? And, lo! the two men found themselves on common ground. All the doubts about faith vanished; the ignorance of tradition was itself ignored; and after five minutes of exchanging rhapsodies on the subject of Israel (the man had traveled there a couple of times with his wife, and was most impressed with the beauty of the land and the nobility of the people), the rabbi pronounced the man a far better Jew than the man had ever supposed, and the man had hastened to agree. Why did the rabbi not encourage this man to expand his Israeli affections into some systematic faith? His column did not confess the reason, probably because the whole business seemed to him self-evident. Others were led to self-satisfaction for the same reasons that this man had been led to self-doubt. The function of the modern rabbi is to resolve temperamental differences, and leave doctrine to another age.

If the parents are thus indulged, then the children, as is their custom, will ask for a little more. Their pilgrimages to Israel are likely to become more serious affairs, their indulgences more solemn. Like my fellows, I grew up hearing of the kibbutz as a wonderful place, an environment of perfect equality in which selfishness is extinct. Although I was not, like so many I knew, drawn to spend a summer on a kibbutz, I was enchanted by the picture; I imagine that even today, almost a decade after Nixon started the nation drooling over the wonders of modern China, the kibbutz occupies a cherished precinct in the soul of every appro-

priately idealistic young Jew. And so, if there are funds
available, he will fly off for the summer on the kibbutz, or
maybe some other enterprise which will put him in touch
with the "real Israelis." Upon contact, of course, the illusions begin to unravel, but this is not a crucial development. The normal American Jewish girl who submits to the
life of the kibbutz, and finds herself greatly belabored there
by an Israeli youth with bad skin and a crooked smile, will
not as a result cease to espouse Zionism. She is quite likely
to feel that her basic love of the Zionist idea has been
deepened and matured by her awareness of the common
bond between Israeli and American Jews. Like every other
pilgrim, she is hoping for perfection but mainly looking for
inspiration, and so she is not too disappointed. The emotional investment pilgrims make in their places of pilgrimage is considerable. One thinks, in this connection, of how
long it took American fellow travelers to admit that Soviet
Russia was not merely less wonderful than they had hoped,
but downright devilish. When the investment is in a spot as
decent as Israel, the pilgrim is even less likely to disavow
his devotional sentiments. There occurs the "willing sus-
pension of disbelief" that Coleridge applied to the reading
of poetry: the young pilgrim arrives, observes, perhaps asks
questions, and, eventually, submits.

Nothing illustrates the strength of the Zionist mystique
better than its incorporation of eccentricities. What could
be, on the surface, more curious than the appeal of Hasidism to a young suburban Jew? There is, after all, nothing particularly Zionist about the Hasidim, a people mainly
notable for the happy stubbornness of their ways and the
malodorousness of their persons. They operate out of en-
claves in several large cities, wonderfully certain of the
righteousness of their lives. Young Jews are drawn to them
for reasons of style and not theology. The charm of Has-

idism derives from its Old World quality; the young American Jew, confronting its heroes and hobgoblins for the first time, feels himself in touch with his grandparents' dusty world. The Hasidim look like Jews straight out of central casting's eighteenth-century Vienna, but they are real, which makes them attractive to searching souls. The attachment to Hasidism rarely assumes the form of full commitment; rather, it helps the young Jew to get a whiff of what he regards as old-fashioned Judaism. Never mind that the Hasidim were never in the mainstream of anything. This is useful to him as he sorts out his life, much as the Israeli journey is useful: both help to infuse Jewish life with a pleasantly sentimental quality. It is not as if the young American Jew desires for himself the relatively harsh existence of the Hasidim, or the Israeli's worries about survival. But if his literal commitments are destined to remain forever American, he is permitted a fantasy life in which his sentimental loyalties revert to the Jewish people and their enterprises. Thus Israel encourages a more well-rounded existence for the American Jew than he would have otherwise. The struggles of Israel involve his emotions as the budget battles of Congress and questions of Rhodesian policy do not.

The whole arrangement is wonderfully flexible; supporting the survival of the state of Israel has become the basic spiritual act of an American Jew. Yet the same Jew has no real responsibility for things in Israel: he contributes his money, voices concern and support, and perhaps travels through Israel for the good of his own soul, but that is about all. He remains free to fashion his own homemade Judaism in America—which permits young Jews of slightly religious backgrounds to drift into Hasidism, and allows such people as the novelist E. M. Broner to create a Yahweh in the image of a woman.

In 1976 La Broner became the spiritual leader of an indignant sorority which gathered for a Seder at the New York home of Phyllis Chesler the psychologist, and author of a recent book documenting her inability to understand men. Also in attendence was the redoubtable magazine editor Gloria Steinem, whose presence provided the occasion with a shiny respectability. "My daughters," began Broner, "I have come to bless you." And so she did, inspired by the God Shanah, whom she worships. "I was their pain, their ecstasy," she later recalled. "I told them that the promise God had made to the Jews in Egypt of a new land was fulfilled. But that the promise of dignity and respect to women was not fulfilled. Then I went around the room and asked them what promises were not kept to women. They said painful things, horrendous things. One woman said she never knew what it was to have a mother. One woman said her teacher was her mother. Another said her mother was Martha Graham. Some said their husbands were their mothers. A large number of us, I also perhaps, felt we were our own mothers and had birthed ourselves. It was a moving evening. Jewish and gentile, heterosexual and lesbian, black and white. The exchange was intense." The response to this heretical nonsense, however, was not. When the words of the Priestess Broner were reprinted in her hometown newspaper in Detroit, only one mild squawk came in reply. It was not as if Detroit Jews particularly approved of the Broner Seder; it was rather that the issue seemed unimportant. "I am an ardent Zionist," Broner had declared in the same article, and that is quite enough for contemporary purposes. Indeed, the idea for her "women's Haggadah," *The Stolen Legacy,* derived from an Israeli pilgrimage in 1975.

And so Zionism has proven itself a tolerant and commodious faith; the contemporary American Jew need do very little to keep his credentials in order. It is of course de rigueur for today's Jew to sound an occasional alarm—to alert the world to the dangers of allowing Nazis to march through Skokie, Illinois, to decry the anti-kike graffiti on bathroom walls, to salute the bogus crusades of the Anti-Defamation League. But in his honest moments of reflection, the American Jew today realizes that the collective profile of his people is handsomer than ever before, and that he owes it all to Israel. Vanishing are the memories of squalid life on New York's Lower East Side; departing, too, are thoughts of real persecution in the European world, as the fin de siècle immigrants rapidly die off. With their disappearance go the stifling rituals, and all that remains is the lovely aroma of chicken soup. The Jew of today is freed (and the younger he is, the freer he is) to create a Judaism in his own image: to shop among rabbis and synagogues, to embrace or deny those aspects of his faith which please or distress him—in brief, to live his life as a Jewish Protestant. The mode is acceptable for as long as he can fix his vision on Israel and merge his soul with its fortunes.

III. ORIENTAL BREEZES

But I have spoken, thus far, of Jews and Catholics, and the United States remains mainly a Protestant land. No mere catalog of the Protestant sects, past and present, can do justice to the variety of religious odors they have provided this republic, and as I offer here no substantial treatise on American religion I shall not trouble the reader with charts recording the rise and fall of the various faiths. It is plain enough to the wandering eye that those who believe Joseph Smith a holy fellow are a flourishing breed, and that those whose faith involves the disavowal of wars are still capable of issuing to the nation an occasional President who will manage to wage them. But what of the vast spaces occupied by Baptists, Methodists, Presbyterians, Lutherans, Congregationalists and Episcopalians? Are their pews as filled as they were the day before yesterday? The surveys seem to indicate that they are not, but church attendance figures are still by no means small. The Protestant orders always functioned best when the community was dependent on them, and so even today they are strongest in the small towns and among the blacks of the great cities, for whom the churches provide the same services as did the Catholic Church for its immigrants, and the synagogue for Eastern European Jews. It has traditionally been best for churches to tuck themselves neatly into a more general pattern of organization, and this has hardly been the tendency of recent years. The YMCA secretaries who incommoded the boyhood of H. L. Mencken have retired, perhaps under warm blankets, with blue-haired librarians who had in their best years refused to purchase naughty books. There is little doubt that the Protestant pastors, uttering the same soothing stuff as their predecessors, lack some of their clout. They preside, as often as not, over congregations in which faith is stripped of the hell-raising qualities which made it more compelling in bygone days. Polite Protestant religion has gone pale in the face.

It was predictable, under such circumstances, that new sorcerers would arise in order to reclaim the more astounding aspects of religion. It is not, after all, as if the human race had suddenly achieved such tremendous advances in the art of living that faith would disappear, save among the hinds who occupy those points on the map that all sensible men have deserted. Perhaps a social worker would believe such things; perhaps a public school teacher. Their own faiths are, after all, often wrapped up in such beliefs. But the ordinary man is forever searching for colors with which to enrich his life. Indeed, his very ordinariness can be measured by his desire to believe in things, and by his secret hope that the object of his belief will prove very great and somehow not fraudulent. It is perfectly natural to want nothing more than to escape into a life of fantasy at the first opportunity. Of course, any man gifted with the slightest amount of sense to accompany his imagination will submit to the tyrannies of biology and economics. This means he does not throw himself at the feet of the newest witch doctor in town, and vanish from the sight of family and friends in search of higher wisdom; he does the best he can at home. If he is an American, with his right to worship whatever he pleases solemnly enshrined in the Constitution and usually respected by the authorities, he will employ his freedom by looking sideways with both eyes; he will thereby discover what people are "into" before he leaps.

At some point he will have sighted a swami, or at least a friend who subscribes to a swami. The oriental scent has by now been inhaled by all sorts of people; their reactions have varied greatly, depending on the degree of escape required by the individual. It is rare to find someone who immerses himself in Eastern religion and does not surface after a year or so. Eastern religion-philosophy (the distinction between the two being Western) is of course no single entity: the lessons of Zen and the Upanishads have less in common than those of Orthodox Judaism and Mormonism. But all the Eastern philosophies have been subjected to the higher American standard of utility. There is, after all, no religious police force to make sure the worshiper has his routines right, and so much improvisation is permitted. It cannot be expected that the Zen of Governor Brown will follow perfectly the example set by a Kyoto monk. The results are often interesting. Zen, for example, is surely among the most puzzling philosophies in the world, dealing as it does with first and last things by repelling the usual kinds of questions. In America this was readily transformed into a revolt against thinking and a celebration of jargon.

One of the nicest aspects of Eastern religion for an American is its disposable character. A couple of years ago I strolled down a suburban lane in the Midwest and came upon an old acquaintance from school days. After a brief updating of the facts in our lives, my acquaintance departed abruptly into a discussion of the state of his soul. Such occurrences are common enough in our day, and so I was not really surprised by this. The fellow was, like myself, of Jewish birth, and so it could be expected that he would find sufficient exercise for his conscience in worrying about the military preparedness of the state of Israel. But no, he was a silent rebel from this cause, and if a Zionist, hardly a boisterous one. He had been, he told me, through a difficult time, in which he doubted the purpose of his life and searched for the secret to salvation. And how had he found it? Why, through meditation, of course! It had helped him to achieve perfect peace and self-knowledge. I believe that I harrumphed upon hearing this, because it only inspired him to describe the nature of his perfect peace and self-knowledge, which required a ten-minute monologue, although his essential point was that the whole thing was simply indescribable. He did, however, feel that the hundred dollars he had spent for six sessions of meditation instruction were the most wisely spent hundred dollars of his life. We parted, and did not see each other for about a year, when we met again under similar circumstances. I asked him quickly if he still enjoyed perfect peace and self-knowledge through meditation, and he looked back at me with a puzzled, what-kind-of-question-is-that expression on his face. No, he said, he was preparing to depart for the great Northwest, where he would prepare to become an oceanographer. Did I know that an oceanographer could earn twenty-five grand a year starting out? I said I had not known that, and I appreciated the information, but, being in a customarily boorish frame of mind, I pressed him further. What had happened to his meditative practices? Wellll, he explained, they had been fine for a while, but they weren't too helpful at the moment.

I have known about a half dozen meditators, and they, too, eventually came to regard the practice as the spiritual version of Handi-wipes, capable of temporarily improving one's life, but lacking sustained appeal. There are, I am sure, a number of authentic meditators in the United States, even as there are subscribers to Zen whose zeal would disqualify them from public office, but they have never been numerous enough to constitute a cultural force. Eastern philosophy's run in these States is due rather to its flexible application, as well as to its relative immunity from the cultural policemen. The guardians of the national spirit are, after all, more anxious to check out the bona fides of an archbishop or psychiatrist than those of a guru, and so the gurus have been pretty much left alone, and the populace has been free to chase gurus in its spare time. Truth-seeking, after all, occupies only a portion of an American's leisure hours; the pursuit of pleasure takes up most of them. When the rumor of Eastern revelations first wafted over Western shores, it seemed as if both tasks had been undertaken at once. So, too, in the later sixties, it was widely supposed that the Bhagavad-Gita was best understood while puffing on a pipeful of hashish. Today, however, it is common to find truck drivers puffing away, and the romantic merger of drugs and Eastern philosophy is at an end—which is not to say that the separate appeal of either is exhausted. The sounds and smells are all around us. The Hare Krishna crews some time ago supplanted newsboys as the loudest voices on American street corners. It was always shocking to learn that someone of notable background had entered the Hare Krishna order—rather like hearing that your barber has run off with the shoeshine boy. And yet, the Hare Krishnas were so successful in their indoctrinations that such things have happened.

My thoughts turn, in this connection, to members of the so-called blue-collar class. My acquaintance with its members is not great. Often I have seen workers at the ball park, where consumption of the local pilsener and the difficulties of the Detroit team combine to produce an atmosphere of beery frustration which presumably does not characterize the rest of their hours. At other times, engaged in the family enterprise of shoe-selling, I have grown intimate with their soles, but unlike the children of many prosperous families, I do not regard myself as an expert on the mentality of the working class. Even so, I was forced to wonder what these folks thought when, a few years ago, they picked up their morning newspapers and read of the efforts of Walter Reuther's daughter to rake the leavings of her parent's estate into the Hare Krishna house she lived in. Walter Reuther's daughter! The man was, after all, no mere labor boss, but a formidable moralist and, as union chiefs go, a character of great integrity. Of course, the workers may have wondered if the sudden plane crash which killed her parents had been what impelled the young woman to her current position. But still the question persisted: Why the Hare Krishna movement? After all, America has never been short of homegrown fanaticisms, and has always seemed more prepared to export them than to import others. But such is the general diffusion of Eastern philosophy around the land that its lunatic fringe, as the sociologists say, has little trouble establishing itself here, sweeping up the daughter of the worker's prophet along its course.

So it is possible today to find a telephone operator who flips the pages of the *I Ching* during coffee breaks. Astrological babbling is on everyone's lips; even people who profess not to take it seriously still expend breath uttering the name of their zodiac signs. I do not mean to elevate astrology to the level of the Eastern philosophies, but its revival coincided with the oriental awakening. For American purposes, these are all separate acts in a solemn circus. The ringmaster is unknown, but probably he looks like Allen Ginsberg. The philosophies are themselves wonderfully accommodating, which will assure them of steadier audiences in the years ahead than the creeds of, say, Dr. Wayne Dyer or the Hon. Howard Jarvis. "Whatever god men worship, they are worshiping me," said Krishna, and, "In whatever form I am worshiped that worship I accept." And so why not Hindu-Christians or Jewish Zen-Buddhists? Why not people who are collectors of faiths, picking among them as their mood pleases? Let Jehovah frown!

IV.   ONWARD CHRISTIANS!

My first strong impression that something new was amiss with Christianity in America came to me in Rome, of all places. It was 1972, and I was surveying the evening parade in the Piazza Navona from a ledge next to one of Bernini's fountains. Suddenly I was startled by the sound of youthful American voices accompanied by guitars. At first I dismissed them as musical imperialists of the usual sort—indignant if the United States pursues any sort of global political interest, but thrilled if it imposes the Bee Gees on a society whose ears are accustomed to Verdi. But soon these voices became louder and closer, and within another minute one of the troubadors had invaded my line of vision. He was predictably bearded and seedy-looking, but otherwise he was unlike others of the category into which I had fitted him. There was a strange enthusiasm to his movement, and a slight dance to his steps. Then the others came into view, and, indeed, they began to dance in a circle, all twelve of them. There were two guitarists and everyone sang. The words, like those of most songs, were full of love, but this time the lover in the tune was Jesus Christ:

> Oh, he loves you
> He really loves you!
> Oh, give your heart for Jesus
> As he gave up his for you!
>
> Because he loves you,
> He really loves you . . .

And on they went, dancing and singing in one place for a few minutes and then moving along to another part of the great oval. The Romans, sitting in the cafés and restaurants around the piazza, did not exactly ignore them, but neither could their interest be described as intense. I am sure my own interest was greater; anyway it was I, and not a Roman, who responded to these tuneful enthusiasts by approaching the bearded leader and asking him what he supposed he was doing. My tone must have been slightly peremptory, as the fellow's reponse had little Christian warmth in it. He sounded rather like the masterwork of some human programmer. "We are members," he said, "of the Worldwide Society of Jesus Christ. We are dedicated to doing His Work and spreading His Word for the redemption of mankind." A fit of impudence overtook me at this point, and I asked him if he really thought it necessary to

do this sort of thing in Rome. After all, was there not a
Pope in the neighborhood? "We believe," he said, "that the
message of Jesus Christ has been corrupted by modernism,
and we include the Catholic Church on our list of cor-
rupters." There seemed to be no point in arguing with a
fellow like this, and so I said something like "Oh," and
asked to be excused for interrupting him. "Not at all. You
are my brother. Christ be with you." After saying this he
rejoined his companions and began another round of "Oh,
he loves you . . ." and I shuffled back to my modest pen-
sione, followed by dark and dirty cats who must have supposed that I had something to offer them besides Christian
brotherhood.

I filed away this incident in my memory as yet another
specimen of American fanaticism, and resumed my pursuit
of less godly interests. In the America of the early seventies, the imported Eastern faiths were still the big story, and
except for those people in the television and magazine
businesses who make a living by watching fads and declaring some of them historic, no one paid much attention to
the latest symptoms of Christian revival. I must say that I
was, after this first incident, more on the lookout for Christianity's soldiers than were most people. I find them curious
creatures, and sometimes more amusing company than my
fellow unbelievers. There was some cautious cheering from
this watchman's tower as the Christian lights became more
visible in succeeding years. About six months after my
Roman encounter, for instance, I found myself detained inside a college dormitory on a great midwestern campus. As
I hastened toward the exit, my nose itching from the attack
of herbal fumes which one automatically suffers upon entering that wild habitat, I was halted by an old acquaintance. (I had once served time on this campus, and
had acquired a reputation for disliking it and saying so, but

a few people tolerated my bad manners and became mildly friendly.) He was still confined to the dormitory, and had little news of himself, so I asked about his roommate, a young man notable for his filthy appearance and prodigious consumption of marijuana. A smile came over my friend's face and he said, "You wouldn't believe it." I assured him that I would, and he conducted me to the quarters which he still shared with the same fellow. Alas, I did not believe it. The hair had been cut, the face, although still savaged by acne, was clean, and the appearance was quite tidy. All this, of course, was believable. Stranger was the cupping of his hands, which held his head in a moment of anguished prayer. It was not until he looked up and gave me a polite but hearty greeting that I learned he had in fact been praying the prayers of a Jehovah's Witness.

And so the signs kept popping up. I would idly flip my television dial upon a weeknight, expecting shoot-outs and hoping for a ball game, and I would find myself engrossed by some preacher in a business suit who prayed hard and long that Mrs. Nosechuck's stomach tumor would take leave of its host. I would return to this program over the course of many nights, when, my spirits having been set low and in need of lifting, I found this program an efficient and healthy alternative to alcohol. It offered me a comfortable feeling of superiority over my fellow creatures. Here were the worst choirs, singing the very worst hymns I had ever heard. Here were the most idiotic confessions: I recall one lady declaring that she had been incapable of square dancing before the night she let Jesus Christ into her heart, and a businessman who said that Jesus Christ had taught him to love "our capitalist system" as it should be loved, after which the host enthusiastically decreed that, although Christ spoke for the poor and disenfranchised of this earth, there was no doubt that He disapproved of welfare chiselers and supported efforts to get rid of them. He even dared to quote "Give unto Caesar that which is Caesar's . . ." in support of his thesis. I was not precisely addicted to the program, but I was certainly charmed by it. Night after night the citizens of this Republic—citizens in checked jackets and striped trousers, citizens in leisure suits, citizens in print dresses, citizens in orange tuxedos, citizens in sequined gowns—would sit before the camera and tell how they came to Jesus. I could of course survive for days and even weeks at a time without the program, but always I returned to it with the joy a child feels upon taking up a game of Candyland. There would be a fresh confessor on hand, sitting beside the same smiling host, who would interrupt to ask a question or supply a cheer for Christ or capitalism. Almost without exception the confessors were completely obscure individuals whose appearance before the cameras may have been the highlight of their adult lives. But one night I was tickled to find a more familiar apparition: Charles Colson, who admitted that he had indeed declared his willingness to trample grandma underfoot in order to secure Richard Nixon's reelection. Colson had by that time served a prison sentence and had come to Christ. His appearance on the program served to expose his latest passion to a wide audience. Colson did this in familiar fashion, by implying that all other passions were inferior and unworthy of sentient human beings. The smiling host never looked happier; he offered an abundance of amens while not neglecting to let the folks know that in Colson we beheld a man who had climbed to the mountaintop and had returned to discover that life was better on the dirt farm.

The Billy Graham crusades never held my attention in quite the same way. Graham was an overexposed figure, the Ralph Nader of evangelical religion, always ready with a declaration on matters within his own sphere of interest, and also on matters not quite within that sphere. With his holy hot line to the White House, Graham seemed a dull echo of the evangelists of old. Yet, his prominence and respectability were symptomatic of the continued strength of hollering faiths across the land. If Graham could get the President's ear, then the yokelry remained susceptible to flashier preachers who knew when to yell and when to whisper.

There were many signs throughout the early seventies that the hallelujah spirit was overtaking the country, but I was no more prepared than anyone else for the emergence of Jimmy Carter, who had had his faith reborn a decade earlier and had subsequently wandered from his native Georgia in order to witness spiritual conversions and hunt for votes. Of course the Carter campaign was not necessarily improved by what Hamilton Jordan called "the weirdo factor," but neither was it spoiled by it; the man won the nomination in a romp, and carried the election. And I, who had with childish delight welcomed the new evangelists onto the scene, found myself dismayed at the prospect of watching one of them roll his eyes in the White House for four years. It had all happened too fast. With Carter's election, the homogenization of the Bible-quoters, inconceivable only a decade earlier, had been completed.

Immediately the itinerant sociologists set to work, rasping their explanations of the phenomenon. The whistlers of evangels now numbered in the tens of millions, there had to be a reason for it, and so we learned that we had entered a new era of good feelings, or that we hankered after a healer of wounds, someone who seemed really different. I was at the time reacting too grumpily to the whole business to think the matter through, but now, after the passage of a few years in which Carter has proven that piety can be as dull a thing as conventional unbelief, I find myself seized by revelations on the subject. The modulated whoopsterism of today is no more than an old-fashioned American assertion of pride in one's ignorance. The grand-children of farmers who gathered in the pastures to whoop with Billy Sunday and William Jennings Bryan now convene silently before their television sets to view those strange confessions, or watch the mild-mannered crusades of Billy Graham. And then, upon a chill afternoon, when the kids are screaming in the next room and the next month's mortgage payment is in doubt, when, in brief, the uncertainties of this life appear impenetrable, a man's contemplations take on a sort of yearning. If, like so many Americans, he has been raised to believe in God and a somewhat orderly universe, and has yet passed into adult life with some determination to avoid the tedious churchgoing of his youth, he nonetheless prefers not to yield those early beliefs. They had, after all, given life a more dignified image than it would have had otherwise. And so, in his moment of doubt, he returns to Christ—but not the Christ of a thousand careful sermons, of theologians and their pastoral interpreters, who only complicate matters more. Complication is after all the very thing he is trying to avoid. He wants to be titillated by the possibilities of belief; he wants the same release for his mind that sex or weekly softball games give his body. And so he adopts the simple evangelical faith which soothes him but does not tax him in any way he does not wish to be taxed. Perhaps, if he is lucky, he will find enough like-minded souls around him to enable him to join a church. If not, he will clutch his Bible and carry on, with a wife or close friend nearby. It does not really matter, because at this point the Word of the Bible is available for consultation. If a preacher appears who can make the words of the Bible march, that of course is dandy, too, but the appeal of his mode of belief is its essentially disorganized quality. The Bible, after all, contains a thousand ambiguities, and a commitment to its Word is no more than a commitment to interpret Christ in one of a thousand ways. And so when a Carter emerges, promising a government as full of love as the American people, the average American discerns no intolerable insolence; each has his own idea of what such a statement means. Christianity would not have lasted so long if it lacked the power to move elemental minds, and the evangelical Christians are mainly involved in restoring an elemental mode to American habits of belief. They are resurrecting the childish aspects of religion and adapting them to the times.

V. THE ULTIMATE PROTESTANTISM

So the Catholics are confused, the Jews are mainly Zionists, and born Baptists are likely to be born again, quite possibly as Buddhists. All of this reduces to religion by temperament. The great questions of religion are mainly questions of style for contemporary Americans. There is probably little intrinsic difference between a true Christian and a true Hindu, but the believers I know are only true Americans. Whether a man proclaims himself a devotee of the Bhagavad-Gita or of the exact letter of the Bible depends upon what sort of image he wishes to project; theology is irrelevant. The American who is born, baptized and buried as a member of the same Presbyterian church is no longer a creature to be taken for granted; he is an assertive character in his own way, declaring a belief in continuity and tradition. He does not necessarily claim that his faith is better than the next fellow's, but he argues by example that it is best to practice the religion which one has always known. Meanwhile everyone else indulges in the current religious

smorgasbord. The general presumption behind all this experiment is that no God is really watching, or, perhaps,
that He is watching and winking. Those with a moralistic
point of view may rightly be concerned; so, too, for that
matter, might those who are inclined to regard all this from
an aesthetic standpoint. Every man finding his own salvation does not appear to be one of the most edifying spectacles imaginable. But it is the ultimate in Protestantism, and
it is fitting that these States should be the setting for it.

5

The Luxurious Conscience

In this great moral Republic, that which a man professes to believe has usually been less important than whether his sense of right and wrong seem properly developed. In times when we are educated to believe nothing in particular and so are capable of believing anything at all, the development of the moral sense has been an issue of special significance. Serious political issues, unless local and having some immediate effect on citizens' lives, will bore and mystify Americans unless they can also perceive a moral issue at their core. When this happens, the American's conscience, otherwise so privately preserved that it may seem invisible, will become galvanized and a riot of images will upset his thoughts. Alarms will sound, voices will wail, teeth will gnash, and after everything settles down, previously cherished assumptions about the world will have been overthrown. The most common occasion for this sort of mind-jostling has been war. This is at least partly because wars tend to last long enough to force even the most indolent creature to contemplate them and to wonder how they have affected his situation. The Great Depression, because of its longevity, invaded American private lives in a similar way. It is reasonable to suppose that all but the stupidest Americans who lived through the Great Depression and World War II had their views of the world affected by them, although it is impossible to take any exact measure of this. The mark of a moral issue in America is the loss of interest in facts pertaining to it. Ordinarily the American is a factual fellow, but when a moral issue confronts him he prefers to dress himself as a poet or prophet, anxious to perceive the inner reality of the situation. Symbols assume precedence; rational debate appears slightly irrelevant and somehow a hindrance to the business of moral purification which has been undertaken.

There have been two great moral issues in the America of recent decades—race relations and Vietnam. Both of these engaged the attention of people who otherwise have all the public spirit of canaries, and so managed to alter their views of life in general, or at least of life as it is lived in these States. Both have now passed out of the phase in which they are regarded as urgent matters; Vietnam has of course ceased to be any kind of issue. The souls of all the greengrocers and graduate students in the land may not be at ease over the resolution of these matters, but not much new is likely to happen. All of this serves to inspire contemplation of the meaning and purpose of these great moral issues, now that the buzzing has stopped.

I. THE METAPHORICAL NEGRO

My family's photograph album contains, among the usual oddities and curiosities, one item which is surely curiouser than the others. It is also more memorable. The picture was taken along a Jamaican beach in the middle sixties, and in it my father, wearing a bathing suit and grinning squintily into the sun, is posing beside Dr. Martin Luther King, Jr., who is dressed in a tie and dark sport coat and is staring somberly ahead. I do not recall whether or not my mother took the picture, but in any case the family audacity was behind the enterprise, and as usual it vindicated itself. It has not been recorded by Dr. King's biographers whether the great preacher minded having his reflections on racism and nonviolence interrupted by a white man unaccustomed to repentence, but I hope that he did not. My father remains an admirer of King, and is proud of the photograph despite his own unspectacular pose in it. More important, the development of the photograph awakened an interest in civil rights questions in one lad of eleven who had been—and, to be honest, would remain—more interested in other matters properly regarded as more important by eleven-year-old minds. It was not as if suddenly I sold all my baseball cards and denounced summer camp as a snare and a delusion, but for weeks and even months I followed the doings of this Dr. King, friend of my father, in the newspapers and on television. I was pleased to hear him roar at southern sheriffs, I thought his rendition of "We Shall Overcome" far superior to Pete Seeger's, and I regarded his public appearances as more interesting than those of anyone else, except the incomparable Senator Everett Dirksen. I had never had anything against black folks, or Negroes, as they were called then, but now I was particularly eager to champion their cause among my white suburban schoolmates, who suddenly appeared to me as moral inferiors. Within the space of a few months, I was swept into the vortex of liberal sensibility.

Sensibilities catch up with people fast at that age; from

eleven to thirteen is one of the longest journeys in the world, but at the end of it everyone seems to have arrived at the same conclusions, and is eager to agree with his peers. My own case—and that of my comrades—was also rather special. The summer after my thirteenth birthday was the time of the great Detroit riot of 1967, and by the time we got back to school everyone was aware that there was trouble between the races. Many, like myself, were members of families with businesses in the city which had been damaged during the riot. I found the riot itself rather exhilarating, something like a war which you knew would end in a few days. There was one lady on our street who passed the rumor twice each day that the blacks were marching out to the suburbs, but we did not take her seriously. We were alarmed, but I was less alarmed than I pretended to be. I wanted badly to accompany my father into the city to inspect the damage to one of our stores, and I supposed that if I behaved like a deeply concerned young citizen my chances would improve. I have no idea if this posture made the slightest bit of difference, but my request was granted, and I was able to observe the National Guard cruising down Livernois, its soldiery looking unshaven and uncomfortable. Down the street the Merchandise Mart had been reduced to a smoking shell. There were shattered windows all around, but I had imagined it would look worse. (Further downtown, it did.) I put on a grim face, handed a pair of shoes to my father to replace a pair that had been stolen from the window, and commented solemnly on the tragic waste of it all. It seemed the right thing for me to say; I was after all being periodically reminded that soon I would have my chance to make a better world, and I thought I should display some recognition that the present world was not good. Of course I did not really believe this.

The riot was the grandest street theater of the time. It is natural that I should think so, even in retrospect, but it was more startling to learn in later years that more active participants regarded it the same way. The original verdicts had been offered with superb confidence; handy ideologies helped in speeding analyses to the city desks. Jimmy Breslin, a newspaperman who transforms into a sociologist after walking a city's streets for two hours, arrived in Detroit and quickly proclaimed, "The civil rights movement is becoming a rebellion." On the other side, the national Republican Coordinating Committee blamed the affair on "hatemongers . . . traveling from community to community inciting insurrection." Americans love few things more than a good conspiracy, and they will work to invent one on the flimsiest evidence. Not a single traveling hatemonger was ever arrested, not even with Jehovah Edgar Hoover bringing the ferocious disapproval of the FBI to bear on the subject. And if the riot was a rebellion, so was the most recent brawl in Jimmy Breslin's neighborhood saloon. The fears of our neighborhood Cassandra notwithstanding, the rioters preferred to incinerate black sections of the city. A year or so later, the Kerner Commission issued its report, which immediately became the responsible citizen's bible on the subject of riots. "White racism," it declared, "is essentially responsible for the explosive mixture." It described "men and women without jobs, families without men, and schools where children are processed instead of educated, until they return to the street—to crime, to narcotics, to dependency on welfare, and to bitterness and resentment against society." All of this was most interesting until it was realized that the Detroit rioters did not fit this description at all: only 10 per cent of those arrested were juveniles, 83 per cent of the arrested adults were employed, and half of these were members of the United Auto Workers—which is to say, among the highest paid workers in the United States.

And so the riot itself appears in retrospect as a messy theatrical, with much aimless yelling and thrashing about. Members of the police force had, it seemed, done their best to inspire the rioters' rage, and some of them could fairly be tagged as racists, but account must also be taken of the natural idiocy of policemen, regardless of skin color. Whatever meaning the riot had was fairly unrelated to the economic situation of the rioters, whose ability to explain their actions was not great. Anyway, what they said about themselves was not half as interesting to concerned citizens as what Otto Kerner's minions were saying about them. It had been that way for a long time: metaphorical Negroes captivated the public's attention as real ones could not possibly do. By "the public" I mean, of course, the white public, and especially the vast numbers of white people who rarely, if at all, had much to do with blacks. Because the condition of the American Negro was a great moral issue, symbols were in great demand; otherwise the necessary understanding could never be achieved.

And so the legends began to form. There were good Negroes and bad Negroes, worthy aims and worthless ones, but in any case they were all transformed by the power of metaphor; yesterday's bootblack was today's man of destiny. In my own youthful circles, it was regarded as a distinct honor and privilege to have a black friend. Once I was seated among five or six boys, all of us rascals at heart but burdened with solemnity at the dreadful age of sixteen. I raised the issue in a tone of innocence: was it really better, all other things being equal, to have a black friend rather than a white one? Thus phrased, the question seemed ludicrous, and everyone laughed; but the laughter had a nervous edge to it, and I gathered that my friends would rather not be laughing about even this minor point. I suppose that in subsequent years, each of them made friends for the usual reasons, and not because it seemed the right thing to do.

The greatest symbol of the American Negro was Martin Luther King, who had imposed himself on the public years before he stood beside my father in front of a camera. He was one of the few great orators of recent times, a man of singularly elemental talents who could not be judged by the standards of ordinary politicians and preachers. Some commentators went so far as to take his ideas seriously, and naturally felt depressed when their burrowings into the man's thoughts yielded little more than floppy sentimentalities. King's thinking, as such, could hardly appeal to anyone with more brains than a high school social studies teacher; the pedagogue might in turn pass it along to his unworldly flock, a few members of which might swallow the stuff whole. The notion of King as a man of philosophical parts never spread much farther than this. I do recall a classmate of mine sitting at his desk one day, actually wiping a tear from his cheek. He was a gentle boy who desired to think well of the world but always seemed frustrated in his efforts. I saw a book in front of him and asked what he had been reading. He held up one of King's volumes, the name of which I have forgotten; they were all slim and presumably pithy. "I was just thinking about him," he said. "He was so nonviolent, so good. I guess he was too good for this world." My normal tone was inappropriate at such a time, and so I kept my mouth shut for a few seconds and then muttered "Yeah," after which I walked him home, and he explicated the wonders of the King philosophy. I was not awed by it. The world, as I was coming to understand it, went unilluminated by such a philosophy. I found my friend's regard for it touching, however, and the fact that six months later he was gushing over some tract from B'nai B'rith did not diminish the impression he had made. But I imagine it would be hard to find a similar instance today; the social studies teachers have by now been enthralled by more recent social documents, such as Dr. Barry Commoner's denunciations of charcoal-broiled hamburgers, or commentaries on California's great Zen Buddhist master, written by a bureaucrat of the third rank and published by Save the Ozone Press.

The King philosophy sounded sacred as long as King roared it to the public. When Ralph Abernathy attempted to fill the air with his own inspired words, it was as if William McAdoo had suddenly tried to sound like William Jennings Bryan after they had buried the old yeller in his barnyard. The message was the same, but the faithful fell asleep. A fair number of King's ruminations had dealt with the subject of passive resistance, but this, after all, was more technique than philosophy; this is at least partly why white people who might otherwise have thought King a nuisance instead tolerated him, and even cheered him on. King's achievement derived from his ability to give his passive protests an overtone of Christian bellicosity. He resurrected, in his fashion, the spirit of "Onward Christian Soldiers." All of this was captured less in the words themselves than in the rhythm of their expression: "Free at last, free at last, thank God Almighty, we're free at last!" "I have a dream . . ." or in that astounding prophetic speech near the end of his life, "I have been to the mountaintop. . . . Mine eyes have seen the glory of the coming of the Lord!" At work were superb rhetorical instincts, with King arousing in people the sensation that they were living in times as grand as those of their biblical forefathers. He was irresistible, and the sound of his voice inspired action.

Even so, his heydey had passed when he was assassinated. He was nearing the point when either he would have had to retrench and mind his business at the Ebenezer Baptist Church, or else become a professional politician. Either way his legend would have dissolved. As it turned out, his assassination was, like Lincoln's, perfectly timed to serve the purposes of mythmakers. Perhaps somewhere in the eternal spaces King and J. Edgar Hoover are having it out man to man, but here on earth the name of King has been etched into the national pantheon, and his image is one of irreproachable greatness.

This, as I say, was achieved by his martyrdom. Once Congress had passed the Civil Rights and Voting Rights acts in 1964 and 1965, King's voice had become less compelling; his oratory had lacked focus. It was very well to yell for "freedom now" and to pass the laws which were supposed to provide it, but eventually anxious blacks—and whites of mournful countenance—could not avoid recognizing that life's burdens had not been much alleviated by these laws. Such redress, after all, was the unspoken desire behind the agitation. If blacks began to vote and even gain public office for themselves in the South, so much the better. But what to do once the laws were on the books? The Negro, in the metaphors of all but the vanishing Ku Kluxers, could now be listed as a full citizen in all parts of the country—and yet his lot remained fairly miserable. The conscientious imagination traveled north and attempted to apply its metaphors to the conditions of northern cities. So, as we have seen, when the riots broke out, everybody had an answer ready. The radicals saw anger on every street corner and perceived great seething on the eve of open rebellion; conservatives alerted the nation to the danger of traveling revolutionaries who would take pitiless advantage of the black man's weakness; and liberals, biting their fingernails, prayed for a flood of dollars to wash away slums.

At least until the riots started, perceptions of "the Negro condition" were fairly stable, and even after the actual situation became palpably unstable, public opinion remained rather predictable. It helped greatly to have Martin Luther King, portraying the Great American Negro, standing solidly in the middle of events and casting his prophetic gaze down upon them. Even if he was as confused as everyone else toward the end, his presence managed to have its effect. But once he was out of the way, the nasties moved to center stage, and the evidence began to accumulate and eventually overwhelm the white man's certainties: there was no "civil rights movement" if there had ever been one. There were only black folks thrashing around in various ways.

It did not take long for Eldridge Cleaver, Stokely Carmichael, H. Rap Brown and other, now-forgotten enchanters to master the arts of sweating and barking on national television, and for a season the scowl of Malcolm X was thought as saintly a memory as King's marches. The appeal of the nasties was for a time considerable. I recall an evening at the start of the seventies, when the day of the black demagogues was already passing. I was at the time suffering through a semester at a great university, and had been diverting myself from unpleasant assignments by conducting desultory research in the affairs of another century. The evening was growing late, and I closed my book and ventured out in search of air and diversion. I happened upon a student of my acquaintance, who had just departed from a harangue by a local black demagogue. He informed me of this without my asking, and then, tugging at his nascent whiskers, suggested that we repair to a neighborhood tavern. I renounced fresh air and went along. My liver was

in those days virgin territory, and I treated it respectfully
by nursing the same beer for nearly an hour. My friend announced that he was interested in talking rather than drinking, and primly ordered ginger ale. No sooner had the bar-
maid vanished than he launched into an interminable
panegyric, proclaiming this black leader a master of political philosophy and oratory, capable of galvanizing white
students by insulting them. This seemed to me a low sort of
entertainment, and after listening to this description of it
for ten minutes I regretted my congeniality and pined for
the open air. So at last, exasperated, I asked him what he
had got out of this experience. He sighed, employed an all-
purpose expletive, and said, "I don't know. But it sure hits
the spot." I praised his iron constitution, and then we
passed on to other matters. It seemed to me odd for someone to enjoy being called a racist, especially when it was
probably not true. But the American collegiate experience
is based on the premise that the student will learn to hate
his parents, at least in some abstract way, and a demagogue
knows how to construct his charges so as not precisely to
charge his listeners with racism, but to isolate them in their
minds from the rest of the world. The result is fairly satisfactory to the listener: by the end of the harangue, he safely
assumes his moral superiority in a wicked world; he can absorb the righteous indignation being broadcast from the po-
dium, and learn to project it himself.

Of course, by the early seventies the general anger had
spent itself. Negroes had by then been confirmed as Blacks.
The newer appellation was supposed to be less patronizing
and more respectful; actually it served to signal that the
party in question was moving out on its own. The old
image of a downtrodden people struggling valiantly to find
the sunlight could not sustain itself any longer. Too much
was being asked of whites, with too many risks and too few

guarantees of success, to keep everyone smiling and singing "We Shall Overcome," and at last whites lost patience with being called racists and being asked to regard reform as expiation. For a time this change was not apparent. I recall a few of my liberal friends asserting, with their usual calm, that those suburban whites who refused to accept cross-district busing of school children, and those who did not care for the "affirmative action" programs were, quite simply, racists. But, with only one or two exceptions, even these fellows revisited their senses eventually; they perceived that the issue was no longer moral, and they realized that facts could be permitted into their arguments.

It was terribly distressing that Sheriff Bull Connor and his marvelous police dogs were not on the scene to assure everyone that the oratory of Alabama in 1965 was perfectly suitable to Boston and Detroit in 1975. But soon it became plain that there were reasons for this. The busing issue, for example, was a farrago of fact and theory in which race, as such, played a relatively minor part. The cases which reached the courts in the early 1970s were sometimes based on the school districts of the late 1950s, before whites had carted out to the suburbs; with the wondrous expediency of American courts, judges actually attempted to punish whites for exercising their option to live where they pleased. Beyond this, parents feared for their children's safety; it was not merely vicious rumor which accounted for stabbings and shootings inside some of the city schools on the busing schedules. American social thinkers are terribly inconvenienced by the fact that blacks commit most of the violent crimes in the Republic,* and some have handled this problem by ignoring it. So, proceeding on the assumption that whites fear blacks for racist reasons, they

---

* Most of them, of course, against other blacks.

reluctantly discovered that sometimes the fear is soundly based and quite honorable. Upon making the discovery, they grow silent; to assert such things loudly in America, even when the span of a great moral issue is nearing its end, is better not done. The affirmative action cases similarly had little to do with race, except in the most obvious sense. Rather, as has been tiresomely argued, it seemed that the assurance of rights had been replaced by the assurance of privilege. One need not be an out-and-out inequalitarian, as am I, in order to find grounds for opposition in such a shift. Affirmative action, moreover, had the odor of class consciousness about it. Americans usually react aversely to such aromas, and this happened here. There are, I know, decent arguments to be made for busing and affirmative action, although they seem to me ultimately unsound. But the point is that these issues have become too complicated to be seen as involving racial morality. Eventually, everyone untrapped by ideology was forced to alter his presumptions. It was not that racism had vanished from the American Republic, but rather that there was no longer any social or political use in pointing to its vestiges. Only a tired demagogy remained. Andrew Young, the lieutenant of Martin Luther King, now elevated to the position of ambassador to the United Nations, detected one nation after another guilty of racism. Looking over Sweden, for example, he found the country filled with "terrible racists." There was a fair editorial splutter after each of his pronouncements, and predictable calls for his resignation, but mostly there was indifference, or at least a general indulgence of this civil rights worker of yore who had come to power and had retained within him much bilge from all those stormy years. The feeling was widespread that he ought to be allowed to get these things out of his system, that he was, indeed, a sort of spokesman for his people;

that all of them were passing through an intellectual adolescence after a long, enforced childhood.* And, lest there was any doubt that Young's fever was spread widely about, the widow of the sainted King soon came pouting forth in Young's defense. The ambassador's comments, she said, had "brought the racists out of the closet." Considering the ferocity of her comment, the reaction was muted. The black man had passed into a new phase in people's minds: no longer history's victim but not yet history's captain, either. Straddled between his past and his future, his situation required much patience and toleration of nonsense on everyone's part. The old metaphors no longer applied. As Richard Simmons, the black deputy mayor of Detroit, said in 1978, "If you asked me fifteen years ago about blacks emerging with power, I'd have sung 'We Shall Overcome.' Now I tell my kids to get jobs where they can get money. If you get out and make money, you can get what you want." The moral issue was gone, and the attendant sentimentalities had to be retired.

II. VIETNAM AND ITS
MYTHICAL GENERATION

Somewhere in the middle of my teenage years I began to find myself reading newspapers with the grouchy impatience I had often observed in my elders. They had been afflicted by the bad news syndrome, and had reflected, in their various ways, the displeasure of civilized men who had learned that "keeping informed" meant keeping apprised of unpleasantness around the globe. I had not yet

---

* Ultimately the Hon. Andy's feckless approach to diplomacy brought him down. His opinions on race relations had not been enough to ensure his return to private life.

reached that point, as I paid no taxes and my affairs were not yet those of the world. Instead, my irritation derived from the chronic appearance of editorials—both signed and unsigned—which presumed to know my thoughts. I speak of those sermons so liberally peppered with allusions to the mind and morals of youth. By the late sixties, the editorial interest in the young became so serious and so severe that I started to feel lost; it was rare to find one attribution in ten in which I could recognize my own feelings. I now recognize the rhetorical purposes of this posture as I did not at the time, and whenever I come across "the young" in an editorial today, I am able to smile. The "youth" of the editorial page exist in order that divisions in society may be made comprehensible by commentators. In this scheme, "youth" is the personification of "change," the presumption being that the older and more settled the individual, the less likely he is to act as the agent of change. There is often a great deal of nonsense in this presumption, but on cramped editorial pages, the symbolism is no doubt useful. Certainly it was so in the late sixties; without the editorial "young," we might never have been convinced that we were living through dramatic and even fantastic times. The ambiguities of the situation would have got the better of our understanding. In the background was the great national adventure in Vietnam, surely the most exceptional in American history. Falsely presuming that if the Communist government of North Vietnam could overtake the cheap dictatorship of South Vietnam it would signal the advance of worldwide Communism, the United States deployed a half million ground troops and scores of aerial bombers in order to resist this development. "The young" were conveniently divided between those who fought (and those who supported the fighters), and those who in varying degrees protested. Here, of course, was the kernel of a great moral issue, as all the capitalized concepts came calling: Patriotism vs. Conscience, Obedience vs. Civil Disobedience, Duty vs. Right, Communism vs. Freedom, and, ultimately, War vs. Peace. Soon the terms of the dispute were being explained in class terms on every respectable college campus: the warriors were captive members of the working class, the protesters were college-deferred members of the privileged middle class. Their protest was not merely against the war, but against the "corporate-military-industrial complex" which had supposedly created it, and to which, incidentally, the protesters' parents belonged. Because these symbols were so necessary to the national debate, there was general agreement on them. Otherwise it would have been difficult to elevate all the catfights over national policy into moral crusades; the full depths of indignation could never be reached; and no one would have felt satisfied, however the war turned out.

The American response to war is as intriguing as any aspect of the country's behavior, and the Vietnam experience was as curious a specimen of this as exists. It was puzzling to live through those years as a member of the mythical younger generation, and it is almost as puzzling to remember them. Early in my teenage years I developed an aversion to viewing the televised carnage. It was not that I was appalled and ashamed by it, as I supposed that war had always been unpleasant and that Vietnam was no worse than others. But I determined that Vietnam was a bore, and that there was neither instruction nor edification to be gained by watching filmed reports of it. I had been raised on tales of World War II, and although the battlefield history of that enterprise had engaged me little more than that of Vietnam, it had at least been a war of heroic dimensions: the enemy clearly needed slaying. But, try as we might (and most of us did not try very hard), we could not work ourselves up over Ho Chi Minh, nor take seriously the Viet Cong in their black pajamas. After Ho died, I could never locate a single person away from a university campus who knew the name of North Vietnam's current leader. Once, in the early 1970s, I stood in a group of solid citizens and examined with them the erroneous banner headline of the Detroit *News* which reported the death of the North Vietnamese General Giap. Each of us took the news solemnly; two gentlemen in black pinstripe suits looked very solemn indeed. One of them said, "I wonder if it will make any difference," and the other said, "Hard to say, hard to say." It was plain that neither of these men had ever heard of General Giap, and neither had the other members of the group. I was slightly acquainted with his name myself, having derived entertainment only a few weeks earlier by reading a radical leaflet which had praised him as a heroic anticolonialist; otherwise the front page headlines evoked no response in me, either. When the error of reporting Giap's death was revealed in a subsequent newspaper, I was with another handful of solid citizens, and this time, desiring to see what sort of reaction I would get, I raised the question of whether or not Giap's resurrection would make any difference. One of the men said, "It's hard to say, hard to say."

It was common, during the Vietnam years, to speak of the United States as torn by strife, with different generations of the same families confronting each other with bitter political revelations. Certainly there was some of this, but for most of the people I knew, and, as I have since gathered, for much of the country, the time was mainly one of general puzzlement. The war served, as wars always do, to distract people from their private concerns, but those who felt in any way passionate about it were in the minority. As it dragged on from year to year, it became more and more of a damned nuisance, and large numbers of the citizenry attached their thoughts to angry slogans. As with the civil rights movement a few years before, tin-pot Isaiahs started roaming the hillsides. By the end of the sixties, the tactical aspects of Vietnam, whether diplomatic or military, served only to entertain retired generals. Everyone else was caught up in the morality of the thing.

No wonder the puzzlement was so widespread: morality had very little to do with the American engagement. It was, and is, generally agreed that as the great Western power of the era, the United States must toss and heave periodically, interfering in other people's quarrels like any maiden aunt with a lot of huff in her. The pertinent questions involve how, when, and to what degree. The Southeast Asian adventure was merely a case of overextension; Vietnam was treated as if it were Austria, and eventually the public's patience with this absurdity wore itself out. Quite plainly there was nothing worth fighting about there. Once Nixon became President, the squabbling concerned the means of disengagement. When Nixon's way seemed too slow and too messy, the yelling started again, but otherwise the withdrawal of ground troops quieted people down. Finally the peace agreement was signed, the North Vietnamese having determined it expedient to agree as later they would find it expedient to ignore the agreement. Then, of course, Watergate came along to take everyone's mind off the mop-up job. The puzzlement dissipated into unquestioning wonder: how did we ever get into such a mess? And most people left it at that. The professional protesters moved on to denunciations of nuclear energy plants, the CIA in Chile, and spray deodorants. Only a short time before, the editorialists had wondered whether the protest of youth signified temporary or permanent divisions in the nation.

All of this, of course, was in the days before the Love Song of Jimmy Carter hit the airwaves. As I have elsewhere indicated, I was a lad preoccupied during the Lyndon

Johnson era. The infamous year of 1968, for others the nadir of the American Republic, was a joyful time in my own life. The Detroit ball club was on its way to its first world championship in twenty-three years, and I tended to view the various political surges, assassinations, renunciations and so forth as a kind of sideshow. Millions around me felt the same way. No doubt my fundamentally frivolous views of world events derive from my ordering of priorities in 1968: it was baseball that had overwhelmed me with happiness, and I could never afterward bring myself to believe that the same ecstasy might be found in politics. Have I been morally crippled as a result? On occasion, I will meet up with fellows who have shared time with me in my youth—solemn creatures, with an impressive sense of gravity about worldly matters. Some have grown beards, and a few, who have retained wire-rim glasses and have treated their body organs unkindly, begin to assume the air of the anarchist Kropotkin. None of them, I recall, was ever much for baseball, and now, as their youth begins to fade, they seem puzzled by the revolutions that never came; they are discouraged by the steady humdrum of existence. They have sought excitement elsewhere, and have found it could not sustain them. I wish them well as long as they do no more than talk, but I would not change places with them. I am still a frequenter of ball parks, still loyal to the same ball club, and although I do not ever again expect the thrill that can invade a soul aged only fourteen years, I can approximate it. And I need not turn my back on the world in order to do so.

For, as I have said, I had early on made up my mind that Vietnam was a dull war, and I had determined to have nothing to do with it. This sniffish attitude was entirely suitable when I was too young to be sighted by a draft board; as the years passed and the war continued, however, I began to grow indignant. It was out of the question that I might lend myself to the Vietnam enterprise, and yet the prospect of conscientious objection was not pleasant, either. I was no pacifist, and I was more than mildly averse to the argument that the Vietnam war was immoral. The North Vietnamese appeared to me a swinish fraternity, but no more so than many others who control the affairs of the world. At the same time, the idea that the South Vietnamese were fighting for their freedom was plainly fraudulent. The choice was between two kinds of dictatorships, and although the South Vietnamese seemed the less dreadful of the two, it was still unworthy of commanding my blood in its defense. Also, as I had begun to hold jobs and receive withholding statements, it was unworthy of my money. But if this left me, at age eighteen, against the war, it also left me politically alone. My prowar friends were mostly boobies who supported the war because the wrong sort of people opposed it. My antiwar friends demanded that I view the whole business as a symptom of the immorality and corruption of the United States, now in the last, dissolute stages of capitalism. A few of my friends quoted the opinions of the linguist Chomsky, a celebrated sage of the day; it was his view that Vietnam represented "a colonial war of the classic type," which seemed to me preposterous. It was not enough that the United States be regarded as wrong; I must also find it wicked. I refused, preferring to retain my own manner of complaint against this vast, inane republic, and so I was accused of harboring prowar, or, at least, promilitary sentiments. Once the question was put to me: Would I denounce the immorality of the war, or would I surrender some of my humanity? Faced with such an ultimatum, I announced I would surrender. To this day I would rather talk politics to my cat than to a college student.

I was fortunate that military service never became an active issue in my life, as I had never resolved what I would do. I was content to denounce Richard Nixon one minute and Jane Fonda the next, but my draft classification would not have been improved by this stirring impartiality. I was subjected to one of the first lotteries, and drew a high number. The angriest among my friends were not drafted, either; in fact, the only fellow I knew who received the call was a waddling pianist who was as fit for the armed forces as Peter Ilyich Tchaikovsky. Subsequently he, too, was deferred, for an obscure reason unrelated to his waddle.

At that point, it became necessary for everyone to cease pretending that the most interesting battles were being fought abroad. Vietnam had in that respect been as odd as any war imaginable. The cliché that war is hell has obscured the fact that war has historically been a liberating experience. Its soldiers have escaped from narrow lives at home into a region of vast possibilities—of adventure, heroism, and perhaps even honorable death. The restriction of life in wartime has most sharply been felt at home, with food and fuel being rationed, and freedom of speech restricted. Vietnam reversed this. The American soldiers who went abroad carried the old illusions of liberation with them but soon found themselves lost in battles that were unremembered, unappreciated and incomprehensible. The unfamiliarity of the enterprise rendered it finally a bewildering and embittering experience. The release this time came at home. There had never been a more prosperous time, and the exercise of conscience had rarely been such a luxury. It was a grand affair while it lasted: everyone imagined that the morality of the Republic was at stake, and so everyone's life became a morality play, fraught with deep significance.

The transition, once the Vietnam war ended and the civil rights workers set up their booths at the United Nations, was not as difficult as it might have been. Without any great moral issues pressing, people simply convinced themselves that their own passing concerns symbolized the human condition. The seventies became the decade in which everybody demanded his rights, whether he needed them or not. Morality ceased to be a word associated with blacks and Southeast Asians; its influence was required elsewhere. Indeed, less than half a decade after the war's end, its most prominent senatorial opponent, George McGovern, was proposing a national intervention (albeit under United Nations auspices) into the troubled precincts of neighboring Cambodia. No one argued morality this time, but instead the senator was reminded gently that his proposal was impractical: the United States had returned to form. The mythical "young" of the late sixties had disappeared in the meantime, not so much by overdosing or even by growing older, but rather through such acts as giving a majority of their votes to Nixon in 1972, like everybody else. In the face of such appalling facts, the editorialists beat a hasty retreat and "the young" resumed inscrutable anonymity. The blacks have made their way slowly, with their opportunities as a race generally improved but their condition generally still miserable. Their leaders talk bosh to the world but apparently we must tolerate them. One hears little these days of the Negro's plight, presumably because there is little inclination to do much about it, such as it is. No one is predicting riots, however; the romance of rioting seems to have played itself out for a while. Meanwhile, the American who was able to strip his own life of undesired strictures by cursing the immorality of war and racism, and hooting for a New Way of Life, is unlikely to resurrect his images of war and racism once he has what he wants. It is much better to forget all that and concentrate on whatever is glittering ahead of him. Forgetfulness ranks among the great American traditions.

6

The Autocrat
of the Bedroom

I. POOR OLD FREUD

I must now disappoint some of my readers. I hoped to
scare off the seekers of cheap thrills. But a few of them,
finding themselves tickled and challenged, have no doubt
read on, hoping that sooner or later I would succumb and
tell the world how I had turned back the odometer and sold
my flivver for ten grand, or worked for a week as a Mafia
hit man. Failing this, it might be hoped that when I reached
this chapter I would include a few tasty morsels which
would make the whole investment of time and money
worthwhile—for this is to be the sex chapter. And yet, I
demur; indeed, I rebel: no salacious tales will come from
me. I am overwhelmed with reticence on the subject;
worse, I am bored with the salacious tales of other people.
It is not that I have retained my virginity throughout a

quarter-century of prayer and penitence. It is not as if I am completely devoid of insights into the human condition deriving from occasions of ravishment. It is rather that I have no inclination to discuss these matters publicly, and I see no point in doing so. An account of my fumblings has as much to do with enriching civilized life as the collected literary works of Nixon administration officials. I suppose there are people who find open discussion of last night's humping both interesting and instructive. I am not one of them. I would rather discuss the situation in Iran. I am temperamentally unsuited to regard sex as belonging elsewhere than in the realm of low comedy. I am open to argument, yet I am uncertain of its relation to the dubieties of love. But I shall deal with these presumed delusions in forthcoming passages. Sex remains preeminently a function, elevated by the labors of poets, quasi-poets and moralists into something far grander and more mysterious. It will not do, of course, to refer to human sexuality merely in functional terms, and to pretend that other elements do not pervade. This would miss the point of human sexuality, which is after all the sum total of worldly sense and otherworldly nonsense piled on top of the function. Still it seems to me as improper to practice public sexual confession as it is to call up memories of bowel movements accomplished long ago. Sex is one of those things that must be worked out by the participants anyway, and so it seems odd that there should be much public curiosity about it. But of course there remains the tincture of prurience behind the clinician's mask, and the widespread private conviction that somebody, somewhere, is having a better time. On top of all this, there is the Freudian heritage, to which all respectable opinion bows.

Amid the enlightened jabber of the "sexual revolution" in recent years, few things have been sadder than the degeneration of the late Dr. Freud's image. Even those men like myself, who could hardly be counted among the rabid enthusiasts of psychoanalytic theory, have found the business somewhat unsettling. Here, after all, was a man of high and mighty learning, a devotee of Kultur and fine cigars, an honest and original student of the human animal. Here was a man entitled to the respectful address of posterity, regardless of his excessive devotion to an idée fixe. And yet, here he was being slapped about by scores of creatures unfit to trim his beard. Men and women of sundry persuasions worked him over as if he were a pretender to chiropractic, or a homeopath who had come in from the cold. Their rudeness has been really appalling. One would think that the fallible theorizing of the late doctor was to be blamed for every sort of sexual dysfunction; indeed, that he was to be blamed for all the sorrows of the world that defied economic explanations.

The observer's pain is primarily aesthetic. It is much the same sort of feeling one would get from assertions by Charles Reich that he sees the world more clearly than Karl Marx ever did; the agony of hearing Herbert von Karajan mentioned in the same breath as Mick Jagger. The sensibilities are affronted; one's dreams of civility are temporarily dashed. There is a momentary impulse to run from the human race and hide. And yet, upon contemplation, one wonders if the offense ought to be regarded quite so harshly. Perhaps, after all, it is only a case of the expropriator being himself expropriated, to borrow a phrase from the gnarled Marxian texts. Could it be expected that inquiry into sexual matters would remain dispassionate? Could it be supposed that the exploration of this primary passion would not naturally inflame other passions? In these democratic times, is it reasonable to assume that a subject of such universal interest might remain the property of white-coated gentlemen? Bah! It is barely three-quarters of a century since the Freudian gospel began to infiltrate the mind of man, but the good doctor might as well have listened to the complaints of the courtesans of Babylon: there has been no reversion to the reticence of previous eras, and there will be none. The subject of sex is now fit to be discussed in the family newspapers. Theories have multiplied, and illustrated volumes on sexual technique are quite respectable Christmas gifts. In the early twentieth century people amused themselves with a sort of vulgar Freudianism, which involved flappers citing their libidos as the cause of lost virginity. More recent muggings of Freud suggest that the current age is characterized by something of another order than this. A more general sexualism is now at work, an elevation of sex to an honored place in the cognitive regions, replete with symbols and solemnities. All the available documentation suggests that, before Freud, every manner of sexual variety and organization had been attempted. The customs of societies dictated variety and taboo in distinctive ways, but to analyze these things would have been preposterous and, in most cases, immoral. When the Freudian armies started assaulting the Victorian battlements, they were armed with a terminology which has long since become familiar to the populace. There is hardly a high schooler in America who is not served the Oedipus complex as garnish for his *Hamlet*. The terminology remains influential, and there are yet many psychoanalysts who can quote it reverently and with more precision than high school English teachers. The Freudians were mere instruments for a broader rebellion. The main business was the opening up of sexual questions; once this was accomplished, the appeal of the Freudians became limited. In the early years of the twentieth century, the psychoanalysts had themselves performed in the rebel's role: the attention paid them divided between reverence and ridicule, with no middle ground. By the middle of the century, Freud's descendants had become thoroughly respectable figures. Barbers and shoeshiners addressed them as politely as they had always addressed archbishops and ward bosses. They were invited to play golf at country clubs, to attend consular receptions, and to organize fund-raising drives for invalid children. Even so, the psychiatric fraternity was never awarded eminence by acclamation, and an undercurrent of grumbling persisted. The biddies who had spanked the psychoanalytic pioneers as a pack of dirty-minded old men had by now vanished; performing the critical function in their place was a vastly shrewder agglomeration of satirists and rebels. Instead of attacking the Freudians on moral grounds, they worked up an intellectual critique, arguing that the Freudians were insufficiently subtle, that they took too little account of social and economic variety, that they were, in a word, unsophisticated. The details of these brawls are not important here. Whether or not the psychoanalysts manage to hold their ground in an individual battle, the various rebels have already won the larger war of attrition: they have kept sexual questions open, and have prevented the Freudians from establishing any theoretical dictatorship. All of this is as natural to science as it is to political life, particularly a science as inexact as one concerning human behavior. The individual citizen is able to enjoy the spectacle however he pleases. He can consult those old frumps, Masters and Johnson, savor the drawings supplied by Dr. Alex Comfort, or read Prof. Erich Fromm's grave treatises on love. Always one of life's main sources of amusement and pain, and one of its chief inspirations to wonderment, sex has now been awarded another dimension through the general liberation. Everyman and Everywoman may now safely regard their sex lives as seriously as they regard their tax returns, their votes for local judgeships and their visits to the opera. No one will think them silly for doing so. Poor Freud! He was a somber man, with a taste for clear themes, but his original chords are buried in the cacophony of recent times. All around are men and women who know nothing of his books, but are convinced that sex is the central aspect of life, first among functions, the source of creativity and depression. It is difficult to imagine this sanctification if he had never undertaken his investigations; it is impossible to consider contemporary life without noting, at least in passing, this pervasive concern.

II. DOWN WITH LADIES, UP WITH WOMEN

But it is hardly the only variation being played on ancient and tender themes. Not long ago I engaged in conversation with a novelist whose books had gained an enthusiastic following without having received the blessings of ponderous critics. His latest work featured a heroine notable for her adventurous spirit, and consequently the novelist found himself receiving letters which confidently asserted his superiority to Shakespeare, Dickens and Tolstoy. In the usual manner of successful writers, he took this very seriously, and did nothing to deflect the compliments. As the fame of his work spread, this novelist was sought out for his opinions on many matters, but editors were particularly interested in his views on the current feminine upheavals. Now I found myself the beneficiary of his wisdom, and I rocked in my chair and listened as he informed me, quite calmly, that the feminist movement was nothing less than the most important social movement to belabor Western civilization in a millennium; that it touched spiritual depths which few people, not even the participating women themselves, could understand; and, finally, that its consequences would not be fully realized for decades, and even generations, to come.

This novelist has not yet entered politics, and his preternatural shyness makes it unlikely that he will do so. But give him a roar and a bit of a lisp, and he might begin a second career as wonderful as his first one. The man dresses himself in the mental habit of the American, to whom the most natural literary form is the tall tale, and the most common manner of judgment is exaggeration. The feminist movement is *not* the biggest thing since Charlemagne, and is probably not even the biggest thing since World War II. Its spiritual qualities are lost on me, unless we have reached the point where X's desire to possess what Y already has is to be regarded as spiritual. One might as well call the New Deal a spiritual movement, or label Jimmy Carter's presidential campaign an uprising of the human spirit—but then it becomes impossible to isolate the transient idiocies of our era, and so I shall have no part of it. The feminist movement, as its leaders will confess in moments of sobriety, is mainly a materialistic enterprise, attempting to equate the status of women with that of men. It is also, incidentally, an exercise in ethical adjustment, but this is a corollary to the main event. In the national manner, this prosaic business has been decorated with uplifting banners; campaigns have been mounted to convince the public that the passage or failure of the Equal Rights Amendment will mark an epitome in the moral history of mankind. This is preposterous: it would mark nothing more than an episode in the long and generally wearisome history of democratic behavior. The debates on this and related topics have been filled with the shrieks and snorts which ordinarily constitute political discourse in this republic, so much so that the novelist-sage may have been correct in one respect: the consequences of the feminist movement may not be clear for decades and even generations. I suspect that when the dust clears and the revelations come, it will seem no more sublime than the other glorious revolutions of our time.

Daily I approach the conviction that there are Americans somewhere to be found who would kick over a dead horse and call it a revolution. What, after all, have the feminists thrown out? The concept of ladies and gentlemen? It was never a comfortable notion in this republic, and became ridiculous once the display of great wealth turned unfashionable. Wealth at least provided for a show of manners—a poor imitation of European aristocracy, no doubt, but still a serviceable model to more humbly situated citizens. Even so, was John D. Rockefeller the model of a gentleman? A country parson grown accidentally and fabulously rich, perhaps; but a gentleman? Or Henry Ford and his lady Clara, lord and mistress of Fair Lane manor on the banks of the River Rouge? An interesting couple, surely; but would ladies and gentlemen inscribe quotations from McGuffey's *Readers* on the stained-glass windowpanes of their home? What ladies? What gentlemen? The whole business was little more than a charade: Wall Street brokers or antitrust lawyers masquerading as gentlemen; the wives of crooked legislators or the daughters of orthodontists parading around as ladies. So along come the feminists, shouting, "Away with this!" and they are regarded as revolutionaries. The feminists did not inspire American women to work; they have done that for many years. The shouting did not begin until the number of women at work was higher than ever. I recall a great aunt of mine, still plucky in her ninth decade, laughing benignly at the report of some indignant comment by a feminist and remarking, "I guess we were liberated years ago and didn't know it." Every family has such aunts with such opinions. The feminists, in their plainest and most characteristic moments, have done little more than demand that women be employed, paid and promoted on an equal basis with men, and that the nation adjust its thinking to adapt to these conditions—a change, surely, but the sort of change that comes at the end of a long process, not at the beginning. This plain-faced feminism, with voice provided by the great foghorn, Friedan, was hardly the stuff that revolutionary anthems are made of. Mainly it was an exercise in useful reform, rooted in social circumstances. It was a case out of the improver's textbook, based on the premise that the cure for democracy's ills is more democracy. In a society without ladies and gentlemen, it was better to eliminate the superstition that they existed: time to stop pretending that the fellow who welded metal for eight hours was Lancelot, and that the woman who cooked his meals was his Guinevere. Such notions had been wobbling for a long while, and they could now safely be kicked in. Raising children remained a problem, but it was not insurmountable, and it was best managed after the deadwood was cleared away. But what, essentially, was this feminism? Mainly it involved the demand of women to run amok in the same ways men have practiced since time immemorial. After all, during the unlamented era of Victoria Regina, women were hardly denied access to the most civilized pursuits—to music, literature, art. The feminist campaign was for entry into far less noble endeavors: for women to become obnoxious district attorneys, stuffy directors of banks, vendors of advertising, or basketball players. It was less a revolution than a Great Lurch Forward.

Changes of this sort regularly occur when the situation

least seems to require them. It was much the same with the racial question. Blacks had been making slow but discernible progress when, of a sudden, great numbers of citizens started whooping for an end to all injustices immediately, and kept at it until changes were accelerated and, ultimately, people stopped listening. Feminists began their most recent campaign at a time when the condition of American women least resembled the circumstances of chattelism so enthusiastically described. If oppression were the necessary precondition for America's minirevolutions, the revolutions would never come.

I am too young to remember any time in my adult life when women did not ponder the extent of their liberation from the domination of men. Some of this has been unpleasant. It will not do to say that one-half of the human race was miserable until an enlightened little sisterhood arrived to awaken it. Most of civilized life has been organized within a framework which the participants have generally found tolerable. It is shallow and insolent to argue that current times represent the epitome of liberty because of the material opportunities being offered to women. Societies have various ways of organizing themselves, and it is premature to contend that the Republic has been greatly improved by the women's liberation movement—that its citizens are any happier or wiser. The actual release of women was fashioned by technology; there would have been no women's liberation movement without washing machines. Housework and the care of children seemed no longer sufficient to fill a life; very well, general adjustments might be made. All things considered, women have adopted all the mundane concerns of men with notable ease, and contention has been fairly slight. As I say, this is the American way of reform: just as women are taking more jobs and infiltrating all areas of society, along comes a mass movement which declares that women should take more jobs and infiltrate all areas of society. The effect is not change, but acceleration; Americans as a people are talented at hurrying things up. Soon the public will tire of talk about the rights of women, and a long period of adjustment will ensue in which the whole matter becomes dull. Meanwhile manners and mores have become slightly tortured, and I, like every other man, have sometimes pined for the imagined simplicities of the past. But to quarrel at this point is as futile and eccentric as arguing that the Blue Room of the White House ought to be redone in lavender tones. I shall view women's basketball with interest and the possibility of approval, and I shall submit meekly to the women in tweed suits who have the honor to reject my loan applications. This is the work of plain-faced feminism, and there is nothing to be done about it.

III. ROMANCE AND THE CONTEMPORARY MODE

But plain-faced feminism is not the whole story. The advanced woman of today is quite unlike the sister suffragette of early in the century. The issues were simpler then; the women who proselytized fit better in the mold of the puritanical past than of our own wide-open day. Some of their spirit survives in the plain-faced feminism of recent times, but the injection of other elements has made contemporary feminism a more potent blend. Here the long-range effects of the Freudian* investigations should be recognized. The solemnification of sex has altered the entire

* And, of course, other studies concerned with sex. "Freudian" is in this case a rhetorical simplification.

feminist recipe, converting clear broth into muddy stew. It was much easier to alter the practical arrangements of worldly matters when the alterations were made within a framework of clearly defined private lives. The solemnification of sex made this impossible; by investing sexual questions with great importance and opening them up for discussion, people have altered the whole idea of romance. This idea had depended on an ideal of womanhood. Now such certainties have vanished. Premarital chastity is regarded as an absurdity, suitable only for nurses, librarians and schoolmarms past the age of forty. Monogamy has become a goal of dubious worth, best left alone until lengthy experimentation has been completed. It might still be possible to dream of a perfect marriage, but it is far more difficult to imagine what might constitute it.

It is possible to carry this point too far. There are of course many people—young, middle-aged, and old—who more or less follow ancient patterns of courtship. I do not refer by this to the chivalric humbug, but something far less contrived: two members of opposite sexes meet and move about on the fringes of each other's lives until at some moment, drawn by a combination of factors not entirely hormonal, they find themselves utterly entangled—what is commonly said to be "in love." It is usually a charming event, so much so that its occurrence is often preceded by deep yearning. It is hard to say which of the two sexes yearns more—even the late Dr. Kinsey and his associated moles lacked the equipment to discover this. But it is my impression that men are as a rule more often moved to action by sentiment than women (although women remain more sentimental on the surface), and that, accordingly, the latest bout of female emancipation has injected more realism into sexual relations. The varieties of feminine behavior that persisted in former times—the nights spent

waiting breathlessly by the telephone, the righteous mainte-
nance of virginity until marriage, the pose of surrender to
the interests of the male—did not reflect woman's sentimentality, but her clear apprehension of the situation. The
arrangements of the world being such as they were, matri-
mony and child-rearing seemed the first priorities of an orderly existence. This belief, cherished for centuries, is still
far from extinct; likewise the belief that a trip to the altar
represents the sanctification of a heavenly match. Such beliefs nourish the human soul, and the best efforts of social
improvers can hardly be expected to wipe them out overnight.

However, it is hard to deny that something has gone
out of romance in recent times—something of its idealism,
as distinguished from all tattered chivalric codes. It is rarer
all the time to find lovers proceeding chastely to the altar;
indeed, the very word "lovers" connotes active sexuality
these days, as it did not for our Victorian forebears. The
rite of encirclement is distinctly altered, and the whole
business of weddings has assumed a more prosaic air.
Under the old rules, the partners in a marriage were not exposed to each other's highlights and defects until the con-
tract had locked them in. Thereafter every undesired dim-
ple or birthmark had to be accepted; every fetish or
reservation had to be accommodated. There was no turning
back without divorce, which at its best was a miserable option. The sexual act was thus reduced in importance at the
same time it was accepted as the essential bond between the
partners. Sex is but a small part of marriage after the early
stages, but in those first few weeks the romantic ideal
would possibly reach a blissful climax. This was made possible by premarital continence.

In contrast, marriage in the contemporary mode is
supposed to be the culmination of a process involving ma-

ture decision-making. Alas, the statistics offer little comfort here. The divorce rate appears to be at least as high for mature decision-makers as for old-fashioned romantics. Life ought to be a steady progress from illusion to the serene apprehension of reality, but it is rarely so. The reform of marital and sexual relations has merely meant the exchange of one set of illusions for another. The old romantic ideal— virginal brides and happily snatched bridegrooms proceeding faithfully into a state of marital contentment—is fairly well washed out. It is now a dubious achievement to marry your high school sweetheart; statisticians will inform you that the risk of failure is high. Disregard of the contemporary mode requires a measure of willfulness.

The newer sort of romance is far more puzzling. It employs the same words, but they have different meanings. In the case of a word like "love," it is hard to tell whether they have any meaning at all. Mainly this is due to the intrusion of explicit sexual concerns. The old, disembodied romanticism of a Shelley now sounds positively ancient:

> I am borne darkly, fearfully, afar;
> Whilst, burning through the inmost veil of Heaven,
> The soul of Adonais, like a star,
> Beacons from the abode where the Eternal are.

Shelley sounds today like a maker of moonshine; his celestial considerations have no part in contemporary romance. It is far more important to recognize whether or not lovers are satisfying each other. This forthright attention to details has made a Shelley obsolete. At the same time, it is possible that the essential aspect of the romantic ideal—the notion of two people joining together to create a more perfect universe—is as widespread today as at any time in the past. The search for transcendent experience remains a persistent preoccupation of humanity. It is now as fashionable as ever for two people to cuddle close together, convinced that they are closing out the cruel world and investing their lives with far deeper meaning than they would otherwise have. If the bodily fluids are called into action sooner now than in previous eras, the difference is one of degree rather than of kind. Part of this is due to the overwhelming quality of sexual attraction, but much is also due to the notions of love which are transplanted from one generation to the next. Along the way, various properties are attached to the basic concept of love. These tend to complicate the process, but they are necessary compensations for the passion which invariably tapers off after lovers come to know one another well. In the past, the mutual interest in children provided the emotional and practical seal for the marriage bond. In large part, this is still the case. But contemporary love provides all sorts of alternatives to child-raising as suitable goals for lovers. It is now supposed to be important that love be "creative," that is, that it promote "mutual growth" in the partners. This is presumably some sort of spiritual flowering that is to result from the implantation of seed.

The ironies are irresistible. In the midst of our celebrations of love, the word which represents its practice is the deadeningly neutral "relationship." This is symptomatic: relationships are love affairs reduced to practical problems. And, indeed, the problems are frequently practical: everyone is unsure of the rules of decorum; everyone wants love to mean more than is summarized in isolated moments of rapture; but no one is quite sure of what love is supposed to accomplish, and it is hard to say when too much is being expected of it. And so the disappointments can easily become magnified. Growth that is supposed to be built into a relationship seems stunted; and love dies, sometimes willfully, with residual doubts about the wisdom of the rupture.

There is always the next day, and new bodies and souls will be available. But a fair portion of life is devoted to searching for the Right One, and distinctions become so blurry that signs of madness can be detected. There is, for example, the singer Lainie Kazan, who proclaims, "I'm not a promiscuous person, that's just my personal taste. I'm a one-man woman, even if it's only for a week."

Those looking for evidence of Western civilization's crack-up often start here, and certainly there is evidence to be found. Yet I am out of sympathy with these righteous critics, for the most part. Human sexual arrangements are bound to seem idiotic in any form; no doubt they are the hobby of a God with a foul sense of humor. But, in contrast to previous eras, our own mismanagement of the situation is relatively harmless and consistently amusing. It is doubtful that the American of the late twentieth century enjoys a profounder and more satisfying love life than, say, an Italian of the quattrocento. But probably it is no worse, either. There is no way to judge. Incredible codes of honor which promoted the fighting of duels have given way to the ethical poppycock of Miss Kazan. However, given the fundamental lunacy of this aspect of life, the relative tolerance and forthrightness of our day seems to me somewhat reassuring. It is better that women can escape miserable marriages to find jobs and reorganize their lives; better that homosexuals of whatever stripe can be left alone to indulge in their own kinds of mating. There will always be complications, and it will often be hard to distinguish between liberty and license, but confusion is preferable in these matters to enforced order—and consequent outlawry. The current tolerance derives from nervous uncertainty about what is really right rather than from the conviction that all manners of sexual conduct are morally equal; it is not deeply ingrained in the American character, and remains subject to periodic reversals. Most people prefer certainty when they can have it, but when the subject is sex it is doubtful they ever will. Possibly on Judgment Day we will be informed that the Puritans were correct to burn their witches, but the risk seems worth taking. Life on earth will be more amiable in the meantime, although it will never be as comfortable as it might be if sex and its various properties played a much less prominent part in it.

It is time to move along. I have held to my promise and offered no record of my sexual past, but now I shall indulge myself and offer an innocent projection of my future. I do so to remind myself that there are a thousand worthy exceptions to every pretty generalization. And so I gaze ahead ten or fifteen years, when middle age will begin to claim me and call me home from my wanderings. Will I seek the comfort of wife and children, and all the trimmings of modest and serene existence? I cannot say. But, presuming that I do, would I tolerate a wife whose concern for getting a living would equal or exceed my own, one who would disappear for weekend junkets and vacate the dinner table in order to resume worldly enterprises? I am quite certain that I would not. Now, I am not the sort of man who demands that his robe be draped carefully over his shoulders, or his slippers slid neatly onto his feet; I am quite content to light my own cigar. But perhaps I shall have to hire a valet instead of marrying a woman, in which case I will know that there has been a revolution in sexual relations, after all.

7

The New Puritan

There is a type of man who worries not that the next fellow is making more money or having a better time than he is, but that he is living more righteously. Such a man is a common figure in these States. He becomes more common as a greater number of people find themselves at ease by the standards of history and other, poorer nations. Once it becomes apparent that there are many ways in which he can live comfortably, he must decide which of these is the best. Occasionally he will wonder how much comfort is excessive; as an American he may well be haunted by the thought that commonness is righteousness.

Such doubts are probably most prevalent among younger people who have not settled into routines; when their youth has been blessed by the wealth of the Republic, their worries will be still more keenly felt. But often the same questions occur to older people. Age is no intrinsic qualification. More important is the lack of any accepted standard of taste to guide the individual toward civility and righteousness. He feels compelled to become a free-lance moralist.

I call this manner of man the New Puritan. His relation to the Bradfords and bluenoses of former times is masked by a series of filters. But the following tentative sketch of him is equally valid whether he is naked or clothed, a fact which may distinguish him from his predecessors in puritanism.

The roads to salvation in our time seem numerous indeed, and there is much room in the expanses of individual conscience where the journey begins. The old puritanism was less generous in its opportunities. Frugality was central to it. Hobgoblins were pursued with a ferocity which today would be considered bad form. Hard and possibly unpleasant work was thought to enhance the condition of the soul. A shrewd piety was in order. Most important of all, the flesh was to be regarded suspiciously, and closely watched for signs of rebellion. The spirit was awarded romping supremacy in the moral hierarchy of life on earth.

The New Puritan is inclined in contrast, to regard his body with respect and even reverence. The change has been so great that "puritanical" might seem an inappropriate term with which to describe the new breed. But this is only because "puritanical" has lately been reduced to a popular synonym for "abstemious." Not too long ago, I was pursuing some canned chick-peas inside a supermarket when I overheard a conversation between two women in the next aisle. They were debating the wisdom of purchasing some chocolate chip cookies. The first woman announced firmly that she would not buy a bag of cookies; the second woman determined to go along with her. They launched into a reminiscence of youthful days, when they would not have considered denying themselves such simple pleasures. Now, one of them suggested, their "puritanical instincts" had won out. (Shortly thereafter I passed by these two women in front of the dill pickles, and learned that, in fact, their common sense had won out, as both were dangerously fat.) There are people who assume that aversions of any sort are traceable to puritanism. Food and sex are two subjects which frequently evoke allusions to puritanical attitudes. It becomes harder all the time to admit that idiosyncrasy and temperament have any place in human conduct.

Yet it is this passion for categorical moral meaning which is itself the essence of puritanical behavior. However difficult it may be to manage categorical assessments of the sundry affinities parading under the banner of "love," for example, more people are making the effort. It is a passion which infiltrates all areas of life today. Consider some of the current diet and exercise crazes. There is nothing new about people desiring to lose weight, and it is hardly refreshing to be told that an hour of brisk exercise daily will improve the tone of one's life. I am an enthusiastic subscriber to such notions. I maintain myself at a lithe and lovely 138 pounds. I am the first man to rise when the cry of "Tennis, anyone?" goes out. I submit to the unpleasantness of running laps around a track, and I worry about my health if I allow a week to pass without lifting a racquet or churning my legs over a two-mile course. I even debase myself in the astonishing agony of weight lifting, in order to relieve a back ailment caused by my excessive devotion in literary duty. Excepting the weight lifting, I have done these things for years, and, if the supreme powers permit me, I shall continue to do them. It is not as if I am some pint-sized Apollo, adept at all forms of athletic endeavor. My tennis is hampered by a bad temper and an even worse backhand; I have frequently been defeated by an octogenarian. I am slightly flat-footed, and my grace on a track only slightly exceeds that of a penguin. Lifting a thirty-pound dumbbell from a rack, I have all I can do to keep from crashing to the floor. Yet, I would not be without my miserable exercises, as I believe I profit from them. I cannot dry myself after a shower without sensing the stimulation I have given to my system. My thoughts, endangered by sluggishness before the exercise, resume their customary brilliance, and I am ready to face anything in the world, even a superintendent of schools.

I am quite certain, however, that my defective moral character is not even slightly improved by these exertions, and it alarms me to learn that some of my fellow Americans believe that theirs are. Tales of redemption come floating my way. Hardly a week passes in which I do not hear a story of a tired businessman or professional man whose marriage is foundering, and who consumes five quarts of Scotch whisky and twenty packs of cigarettes each week. He consults a physician, who affects grave concern, and then commences jogging at an hour of the morning when only farmers are awake. Before long he is running five to ten miles daily. He throws away his cigarettes in disgust, drinks nothing stronger than fruit juice, and soon he and his wife are enjoying the bliss of honeymooners. His life is filled with meaning and purpose again, and he will now proceed toward the grave with a serene, Christian smile upon his face and beads of sweat upon his brow. It is a scenario encountered with some variations in the newspapers, magazines and paperback books of our day. The author of the description is usually some physician who makes money from the resurrection. He does not bother to mention that his patient must objectively be accounted a fool and a mere exchanger of intoxications.

Even so, he has prophets thundering on his behalf.

Several months ago I was listening to my radio when a mature and unfamiliar voice informed me, "Every day I run I am born again." And then a voice-over declared that "running may be the greatest experience you'll ever know." My running shoes were nearby on the floor. I stared at them and wondered what these people could possibly be talking about. A few days later I was looking over the dull pages of a book review section in a great metropolitan newspaper. Suddenly I noticed a review of a new book on running. There was something familiar about the quotations. Could it be? It was: the radio announcement of one man's reincarnation in a track suit had been a commercial message for the book. And here were further quotations from his gospel: "When I run the roads I am a saint. I am Assisi wearing the leanest and meanest of clothes"; "I am a descendant of . . . people of the mind. Men like Kierkegaard and Emerson and Bertrand Russell"; "I am who I am and can be nothing but that"; or, best of all, "Today I took Truth and ran with it on the Ocean Road." The least astonishing thing about this prophet was his Irish ancestry. Somewhat more curious was his status as a licensed physician, a breed whose idealistic tendencies normally remain submerged except upon examination of stock portfolios. But the only thing which made these facts notable was the fabulous success that the doctor enjoyed: hundreds of thousands of books in print, perhaps millions of people eagerly investigating his thoughts and wondering if they ought to adopt them for themselves. Even in a nation with an insatiable appetite for respectable fools, this was a remarkable development.

About a century ago the English endured a craze in which physical fitness was equated with virtue, but the current American follies have a distinctive twist. The loosening of sexual behavior has had much to do with it, so that, at times, the New Puritan can appear downright Dionysian. Any patron of discotheques can see this for himself. Here the intention is a general release of energy, following the absorption of rhythmic noise. In raising such matters, I enter dangerous waters, like a citizen of Delaware dipping his toe into the Amazon. But my experience of revelers is sufficient for me to recognize the categorical overtones which have penetrated the noise. There is talk of the "negative energy" of the daylight hours being firmly replaced by the "positive energy" involved in the abandonment of the body to the disco beat.

On the general subject of dance, another sign of the New Puritan's high regard for the body is found in the rise of the balletic art to high prominence over the past decade. Here, too, my immune systems restrain me from extensive commentary. It seems to me a far greater pleasure to hear any competent orchestra play a single Schubert symphony than to observe the most superb anti-Communist gazelle go leaping to the third-rate strains of *Coppelia* or *The Sorcerer's Apprentice*. Much of "modern dance" seems to me no more amusing than the stretching exercises of my plumber's wife. Of course she is a woman of Maltese extraction, with unusually round and dimpled arms, and I have had only a single opportunity to witness her in action. But at least she had Mozart on her stereo. The last time I saw a modern dancer, she was attempting to create beauty with the inconsistent blips of John Cage in the background. Yet some of my most charming and intelligent friends would disagree with me.

Categorical meaning has even crept into the language of locker rooms. Instead of praising athletes who play hard, coaches are now pleased when their charges perform "with intensity": a little tastier, a little more meaningful. For the first time in recent memory, there is wide interest in the bulging attainments of body builders, the idea being that these men have realized a physical perfection which signifies a sort of human perfection.

But puritanism of the older or newer variety cannot exist without guilty consciences. The New Puritan's corporal preoccupations are consequently reflected in the generalized hypochondria of our time. In an age when more people are living longer and enduring fewer obscene diseases than ever before, the preoccupation with the subject of health is at an unsurpassed level. There is relish taken in the subject of cancer, which remains the most mysterious of common deadly diseases. No item in the news is more likely to prompt excited discussion at the dinner table than the revelation of yet another cancer-causing agent in the air, water or food. After five minutes of breathless exposition and argument, there will be a round of headshaking as everyone concedes that soon it will be impossible to eat, drink, or breathe, and feel safe afterward. Among the magicians of metaphor, "cancerous" was for a long time accepted as a synonym for "unpleasant." This practice was, however, recently abolished by Miss Susan Sontag, who was applauded as a heroine for her essay in stern reproof. The discovery of "legionnaire's disease" may now provide metaphorical relief. Wherever Mr. Norman Mailer was once inclined to denounce skyscrapers as cancerous, he might now declare them pneumonic with much less sacrifice to the literal truth.

And so the body, which once inspired simple fear and loathing among old-fashioned puritans, now evokes a more complicated response of reverence and worry among the newer breed. The evidence indicates, however, that the reaction is basically as superstitious in one case as in the other. If the scientific spirit were behind the change, then people would calmly accept word that cancer is, of all diseases, essentially the most natural, however subject to environmental aggravation it might be; that exercise is no surer cure for meanness than drink; that sex is only sex, and the human body only a body, their possibilities as instruments for human improvement having been exhausted long ago. But the New Puritan is convinced that he can transcend himself from within himself, which is why he refuses to acknowledge these limitations and regards cancer with such fascination. His belief in self-transcendence and fear of self-destruction inspire him as he makes his daily rounds.

He goes in search of nature. As I remarked earlier, the American regards himself as the natural man, called into cities by necessity but never completely at home there. In his places of residence and places of leisure, he indicates where he prefers to be. In recent years this preference has become flagrant, with all the whooping for the natural life. For a time it was thought to be a passing fad, but lately it has seemed that the current version of the back-to-nature movement has more staying power than skeptics initially credited to it.

It has not been merely back to nature, but back to the roots wherever they may lie. This might involve Alex Haley listening to the mumbles of Gambian tribesmen, or young Americans of Polish ancestry organizing folk dances in Hamtramck. The pining after roots and nature is the American variation of a worldwide effort to rescue personality from the snares of technological life. The pan-Islamism of the Middle East and the nationalistic fevers of small nations are comparable happenings. The voluptuous abundance of American life tends to restrain such proceedings here. Instead of denouncing imperialism and organizing jihads against its artifacts, the American can be content with reassurances from beer companies that his beverage is naturally brewed and contains no artificial preservatives. He can also patronize health food stores, where unattractively packaged and unpleasant-tasting items are sold at exorbitant prices. The sacrifice on behalf of naturalness seems worthwhile.

He will attempt to live as close to nature as possible. In former times it was expected that a young man of normal ambition would carry himself off to one great city or another in order to make his fortune. But among the friends of my youth, a fairly representative bunch, such ambition characterizes a minority. I would estimate that maybe two in five aspire to the glory of civic success; the rest are interested, in one way or another, in composing themselves in some natural setting. A former star of the high school football team declared that he was tired of exploitation by football coaches, resigned from his college team, and took up tree-chopping in Oregon. His former teammate informed me he was tired of city and suburban life at age twenty-three, and was traveling to northern Michigan where he hoped he would discover a bar in need of tending. The difference is between sensibilities, not levels of intelligence. I think of one friend, a cherubic character whose sense of humor was as grand as any I have known. In his youth he mastered the bassoon, and entered one of the finest music schools in the land. But soon he tired of the competitions organized by music professors, and lost all appetite for impressing orchestral bigwigs. So he removed himself to the Michigan countryside and began the life of a farmer. Today his bassoon is played only for his Elsie, in reward for a well-filled bucket of milk. Admittedly this is a rare case. Most of my old friends are merely drifting and seeking the proper blend of righteousness and prosperity. This fellow has unusual integrity, and does not care what the world thinks of him.

A true New Puritan, in contrast, cares very much. Consequently, overt ambition has fallen out of style. The spirit of the go-getter is now commonly regarded as vulgar. The Texan, who once symbolized this spirit, has become a weak joke to the rest of the nation, and inspires snickers as soon as his back is turned. The most widely admired capitalists are not the chairmen of General Motors or IBM, but the proprietor of a cute new restaurant, or the keeper of a candle shop. The making of money has become less important than the making of style. The man who leaves a large construction firm in order to enter business for himself earns grudging admiration for his independence, but the dropout from I.T.T. who organizes an organic food cooperative may become a cultural hero. Yet there is nothing more than a stylistic difference between them.

In any case, the inchoate yearning for nature reflects a restless drive for creative independence. It is likely that more bad poetry is being written, more unappealing pictures are being painted, and more banal songs are being composed in the United States today than ever before. Public encouragement is given to this grave dilettantism by the National Arts Council, which subsidizes the efforts of deaf old ladies to learn painting, and the construction of dusty booths by Choctaw potters attempting to sell their stuff. Many who are too lazy to write or paint satisfy their creative yearnings by contemplating and reciting the turgid homilies of Robert Pirsig and Carlos Castaneda.

I am not as sympathetic to all this as perhaps I should be. Laboring as I do with words and typewriters, I am required to spend more hours alone than most people. It is a situation against which my instincts frequently rebel. Often I feel tempted to rise from my desk and walk out onto the street, grabbing the first person I see and exchanging heated denunciations of such beloved institutions as the

President of the United States, the New York *Times*, and the Hon. Bowie K. Kuhn, commissioner of baseball. Usually I suppress these lurid fantasies by pacing the room for a few minutes and then returning to my work, plodding on until the day's portion of wisdom has been indelibly stamped on three or four pages of paper. I am, in brief, a naturally gregarious fellow sentenced by my craft to be more of a loner than I would otherwise be. It is a sentence I willingly serve, as it has its compensatory satisfactions. I simply do not contend that it is completely allied with my nature.

In reflecting upon this, I grow aware of the disparity between myself and most of the New Puritans I know. I am, after all, engaged in business which they freely term "creative"—that is, I am enslaved to no master, I may come and go as I please, and my work encourages me to express my thoughts and feelings without much deference to the wishes of others. And yet, I am numbed and even embarrassed by any reference to my "creativity." It is not that I wish to be known as the professional equivalent of a bricklayer or a scullery maid. I am delighted to think that I am engaged in a superior sort of enterprise. But beyond this elemental pride, and a hope that I will be thought competent, I cannot imagine what other people's notions of creativity have to do with my daily labors. I do not suppose that the craft of writing is in itself more civilized than a dozen other pursuits; nor that it provides more outlets for the imagination, or opportunities for the higher sort of cunning. It is, moreover, as enveloped by habit as any other manner of work—so much so, in fact, that a professional writer can be picked out from any crowd of mangy scribblers by his ability to say "humbug" to all notions of creativity and its little sister, inspiration.

All this has been said before, and I resurrect it only to

assist in the illumination of a contrast. These New Puritans are not dull and dumb, although they tend to be crippled by an unhealthy strain of idealism. Even so, they are at least as much in touch with humanity as I am, whether they are students preoccupied with the recondite passions of academia or men and women of the world, drawing paychecks and faithfully filing Form 1040 with the Internal Revenue Service each year. It is hoggish and Wolfean to speak of these people trying to "find themselves" (oh, lost, and by these words never located!). But they lack my strong sense of vocation, and so I am never completely at ease among them. I cannot imagine what I would do if some magistrate ordered me to continue through life without paper and typewriter, much as Mr. G.M. would be aghast at being told he would have to work in blue jeans instead of baggy suits, and would have to dirty his hands daily instead of filing papers in the dull glare of a fluorescent light. My "creativity" is but a mask for self-enslavement, and I know that on weekday mornings I must report to my blank sheets, even if no literal obligation exists.

In contrast, the New Puritan has freed himself from all this. He may report to work each day, but he feels no permanent loyalty to the work being done. As captain of his body and soul, his obligation is not to a job, or a boss, or a company, but to life itself. He will decide which form of activity is most righteous before he undertakes it. His sense of duty is stripped down to a feeling of complete responsibility for himself. He convinces himself that if he handles it right, he can make of his life a work of art with high moral content.

I confess to a pagan's prejudice: art for art's sake seems to me a sensible doctrine, but art for life's sake sounds a trifle desperate, and life for art's sake is utterly preposterous. The idea makes no more sense to me than life for God's sake, around which, after all, many wonderful theologies have been constructed. But the New Puritan is deeply concerned with the sort of work a man does; he does not concede equal dignity to all forms. The moral qualities of anyone who goes to work for General Motors, for example, are presumed to be in deep trouble. His sense of right and wrong is endangered by the corporate juggernaut. The principles of the righteous life will be compromised, and the opportunity to convert earthly existence into an act of moral art will probably be wasted.

Perhaps they are right; certainly corporate life affects a man's character, and maybe corporate life in itself is responsible for whatever moral lesions separate man from his ideal state. But I do not think so. It seems to me that the groundhogs of humanity are as adept at finding their holes as the groundhogs of nature. The corporation inherits the personality and, if anything, perfects it. The issue may be viewed without indignation or the milder forms of moral anxiety.

Once, during my student days, I was strolling through the campus with a friend. He was dubious of the value of the university for moral purposes, and talked of dropping out in order to hitchhike through Europe or attempt to live off the land. He was a passionate boycotter of grapes, and considered, for a time, the possibilities of migration to California, in order to assist in the unionization efforts of the sainted Chavez. He dressed in flannel work shirts and jeans, and proclaimed the superiority of marijuana to all forms of liquid refreshment. His girl friend wore peasant smocks and disdained bras. Together they could achieve deep fervor on the subject of the military-industrial complex. His sense of humor, although endangered, was still sufficient for me to find his company pleasant, but plainly he took himself and life in general quite seriously—perhaps to a degree that only people living the academic life find possible.

As we walked, I introduced the name of Beethoven into the conversation. I spoke of my unbounded admiration for the man and his music, for the forthrightness of his effort, and for the tremendous dignity of his life. My friend was no philistine, and he hastened to announce his appreciation of Beethoven's music. But otherwise he was skeptical. "What was so great about his life?" he asked. "He quarreled with the only friends he had, and he did not have all that many. He never married and probably had a lousy sex life. He was a lonely and unhappy man. You can have his life." I responded that I should gladly toss away the mundane joys of my own existence in order to attain the majestic pleasure of composing those symphonies, sonatas and quartets. But my friend remained unimpressed.

Here was the division between me and the New Puritans, although in the enthusiasm of my late teens I may have carried the argument further than I would today. He could not envision the complete immersion of oneself in one's work, whereas I could see no other possibility. He saw work, even of the "creative" variety, as useless unless it yielded spiritual rewards manifested in personal happiness; I saw it as an inevitability to be embraced and then mastered. If he were to organize grape pickers, or work off the land, he would be doing so not primarily because the work was absorbing, but because it was good for him. I had no idea what this meant.

It is of course possible for a professional in any category—artist, doctor, piano tuner—to be a New Puritan at heart; I suspect that it is likelier all the time. It then becomes difficult to gauge the factors which motivate him. Nevertheless the division is clear. The professional reaches toward some ideal of competence—he may give it a more exalted term—which, if achieved, would satisfy him. He has the facility for detachment and his standards are objective; those of the New Puritan are subjective.

All of this lends an eccentric quality to contemporary life. For every thousand anonymous examples of New Puritanism there will be a famous one. A star basketball player, paid hundreds of thousands of dollars per season, decides suddenly to abandon his team in order to drive a taxicab; he imagines this will bring him into touch with the real world. The wife of the prime minister of a great Western nation proclaims that she still loves her husband but must leave him in order to fulfill her destiny by photographing rock musicians. All prior claims of order are set aside, replaced by private visions of happiness.

The Great
March Forward

I. NOSTALGIA FOR THE SIXTIES

Not long ago I broke bread with a young man of seventeen, whose life was still burdened by the vacant assignments handed down by high school teachers and by the other horrors of adolescence. He was a smart fellow with a wide range of interests, and I was happy to assure him that the days ahead would be happier for him. I have yet to meet a single above-average person whose teenage years were not filled with nameless and unreasonable terrors, and so my counsel was easily and confidently given.

Soon our conversation turned to subjects of general interest, and landed upon politics. Although I do not customarily risk disorderly digestion by discussing such topics at mealtime, I was sufficiently charmed by this fellow to permit his thoughts to pass before me. The big question, he

said, is what form American politics will take in the 1980s.
He despaired to think that they would be as dull as those of
the 1970s; the eighties, after all, would be *his* decade, and
one was entitled to hope that these years would amount to
something. I did not mention my distaste for the national
preoccupation with decades and generations, but instead
asked him to outline his hopes. A scowl covered his face as
he considered the question. In a few seconds he answered,
"The sixties. All in all I think it would be nice if the eighties were something like the sixties."

The sixties! Ah, yes. My wide-eyed years. But what
did he mean? Another Kennedy presidency, filled with yapping about a New Frontier and the joys of national health
insurance? Another idiotic overseas adventure, inspiring
widespread distaste and revolt? Another revival of protest
ballads by Joan Baez, with wheezier renditions by Pete
Seeger? More marches on Washington with Norman
Mailer? The return of Walt Whitman Rostow to "Meet the
Press"? But I am being playful. I knew what he meant, and
he knew that I knew, and so we smiled at each other in the
manner of two conspirators contemplating arson.

He desired a mood, not a policy; an atmosphere in
which the American masses would rise up to howl at the
cowardly stupidity of their leaders. Despite the decrepi-
tude which overtakes you after a quarter-century of life in
these States, I could feel the stirrings of sympathy within
me. As one who has long believed in public whippings of
bad governors and has accepted with the deepest regret all
the arguments against life imprisonment for Richard
Nixon, I am naturally alert for all the rumors of rebellion in
the land. The later sixties were years of largely incomprehensible revolt, and their spirit passed me by in many
ways, as I have indicated elsewhere. But I am always hope-

ful and watchful, and I am always more encouraged by seventeen-year-olds who believe the situation could use a smashup or two, than by those who believe this is the best of all possible republics in the best of all possible worlds.

But in contemplating my younger friend I could not help but feel a little sad. He was, after all, in the midst of being presented a world in which there was hardly a taboo worth violating. It seemed a great shame. What is the point of being young if you are bound to be tidier than your elders? Hence the air of amused and slightly resentful resignation that I find among many in their late teens and early twenties these days. It is quite wrong to suppose that the country has resumed clicking along on Eisenhower time. Even as the work of the world gets done, the search continues for objects worthy of defiance, symbols of stupidity for a generation to hang its hat on.

II. THE UMBRELLA OF TOLERANCE

In the meantime, the New Puritanism flourishes. A vast umbrella of tolerance now covers the life of these States. Its expansion was first visible toward the end of the Vietnam years, when it became evident that all the shouting was quieting down, and yet there was no reversion to the buttoned-down days of old. Instead, the multiple ironies of American life were chasing the citizens toward doubt. The laborer knew that he could not claim to be a victim of sweatshops; the businessman knew that neither approval nor disapproval of him was complete; the independent man was forced to realize that his freedom may not have brought him happiness. As the sons of affluence, required to assemble their virtues, they adopted tolerance as their first principle of behavior. Not approval, by any means, but simple tolerance. It was a tactical move which helped them to find their way.

The Supreme Court of the United States respectably epitomized this tolerance in its consideration of the case of Cohen *v*. California. The appeal had been made by young Cohen after his arrest and conviction for disturbing the court of Los Angeles County by strolling through the courthouse wearing a jacket which featured the inscription "Fuck the Draft." The late Justice Harlan, speaking for the majority, did not merely overturn the conviction, but enunciated a principle for our times. "One man's vulgarity is another's lyric. . . ." This presumption has been behind most of the public thought on American cultural life in recent years. Tolerance of diversity has been so great that when the issue of the First Amendment is raised in court these days, the subject being debated is invariably some utterly revolting form of human expression. The rights of pornographers and Nazis are all that remain to be fought about. Everything else is automatically awarded the official seal of approval. The civil libertarian, once engaged in heroic battles on behalf of James Joyce and D. H. Lawrence, must now content himself with Sidney Smut and Harold Hitler as the representatives of his lofty and indignant principles.

Only in the past couple of years, when the doctrine of tolerance flowed at high tide, has there been any whispering of second thoughts. There was the amusing case of Mr. Larry Flynt and his *Hustler* magazine, surely one of the most repellent journals ever sanctioned by a civilized society. Here were the minions of Flynt, dashing up and down the highways of the Republic, signing up defenders of liberty by the hundreds. Here was one great mind after another, invoking the wisdom of Voltaire and babbling about not agreeing with what you say, but defending to the death your right to say it. Here were proclamations that a great moral and legal issue was at hand: Harvard professors despairing of the nation's future if poor Flynt went down; high and courtly authority worrying darkly about the precedents that might be set; officers of local police forces waiting eagerly for word that they could proceed to raid and close down evil newsstands. But then—slowly, almost inaudibly—low growls were heard in some of the most forward-looking precincts on the island of Manhattan. A swarthy feminist announced that free speech could be hanged, she would have no truck with Flynt and his degradations of women. A svelte feminist served up the same message in cooler tones. Finally a host of magazine editors began checking in with their doubts. One of the most eminent among them went so far as to suggest that *Hustler* may not have been what our Founding Fathers had in mind when they drafted the Bill of Rights. Before long the enthusiasm for the issue had been dissipated, the Flynt case was ruthlessly demoted on the roster of great moral issues facing the nation, and the embattled publisher was left alone to face his unhappy destiny.

Such incidents only show that fashionable tolerance can reach its limit, not that there is any great leap backward going on. Save among the sourest specimens of American humanity, tolerance is a cherished and enjoyable principle. No rigorous thought is required to defend it, little is demanded of its adherents besides a limited generosity of temperament, and ample room is left for self-righteous display. The last of these attributes may well be the most significant. Where all questions can be ultimately reduced to a matter of individual, unenforceable opinion, everyone may properly proclaim the superiority of his own views. This results in a kind of chaos, but what is democracy if it is not chaos domesticated by institutions?

III.   THE FLIGHT OF THE BUGABOO

Yet this tolerance has thrown up a serious impediment to the progress of democracy in America. It threatens a severe shortage of national bugaboos. The character of an American bugaboo is simple: it is something which a large number of people believe is disturbing or even poisoning American life to an intolerable degree, and which therefore must be eliminated. The chasing of bugaboos has always been the supreme national pastime, surpassing baseball in antiquity and in the fervor of its practice. Large groups of angry citizens march through the corridors of American political power, organizing petition drives to put the issue on the ballot, attending rallies which feature speakers slobbering with rage, marching on Washington and camping out on the Mall, writing subliterate pamphlets, and otherwise fashioning imaginative methods to stir their fellow citizens out of complacency. The bugaboo hunter is often inspired by memories of the patriots of the Revolutionary War era. He remembers that only a third of the colonies' inhabitants favored sending King George his walking papers. Even if his historical memory is short, the bugaboo hunter is firmly convinced that the elimination of his bugaboo will render America the greatest imaginable service in purifying its pursuit of heaven on earth.

But the bugaboo hunter does not act alone and uncontested. There are always those who represent the bugaboo, as well as those who represent neither party in the dispute but are simply offended by the bugaboo hunter's style. The bugaboo hunter, in his turn, finds support from those who resent the style of those who resent the bugaboo hunter . . . but I do not presume to remodel the house that

Jack built. I state simply that various parties are thus engaged in the bugaboo hunt, and the spirit of the nation is amply exercised.

American life in the twentieth century—to confine ourselves to easily remembered history—has been greatly enlivened by bugaboo hunts. A couple of old examples are Prohibition and the Red Scare cooked up by Attorney General A. Mitchell Palmer at the end of the First World War. In each case the bugaboo hunters were absolutely certain that the elimination of their bugaboos—alcoholic beverages and Bolsheviki—would purify and uplift the life of the land. Leaping over a few decades to the age of enlightenment which commenced with the dropping of atomic bombs over Hiroshima and Nagasaki, we find a rich assortment of bugaboos entering American life. In order to avoid charges of partisanship, I recall a favorite bugaboo of each political wing in that era. The rightists, preempting the priorities of the old liberal, Palmer, revived his Red Scare in the form of McCarthyism. A hundred dull books have pointed out that this involved the pestering of numerous individuals in and out of government, who were suspected of having had youthful infatuations with the thought of Karl Marx, and of having displayed regrettable tolerance of Marxian operatives in subsequent years. McCarthyites rejoiced in what must be accounted one of the most glorious bugaboo hunts in American history. Despite a remarkably low percentage of accurate accusations by McCarthy himself, the exhilaration of the chase must have provided satisfaction enough. It was delightful to suppose that the Republic was being purified after its having been so evilly tainted.

In the same decade, the left wing took up the cry for the unilateral renunciation of atomic weapons. The most famous participant in this bugaboo hunt was actually an

Englishman—Bertrand Russell—rather than an American; it may be fair to suppose that like so many of our national practices, bugaboo-hunting is of English origin. In this case it was widely presumed that an American initiative would inspire the Russians to behave similarly, and that the life of the entire world would be uplifted.

The 1960s were distinguished as a great age in the history of the American bugaboo. Almost every month would bring forth some confusing new matter which would bring out the bugaboo hunters in droves. To list Vietnam, racism and marijuana is to list only the most obvious examples. As the sixties slipped into the early seventies, the flow of bugaboos continued unabated. There were more isms to shout about, sexism most prominent among them. There were abortion, homosexuality, pornographic movies, Richard Nixon—fine bugaboos all. The populace became really riled, opposing factions routinely accused each other of being traitors, and the public atmosphere was amusingly bilious.

But lately one notices a change. Not since the days when Coolidge snored in the White House have Americans seemed less inclined to mount barricades and proclaim sure cures for all the sorrows of the world. This might be great news if we were talking about some other national variety of human being, but the American, as every intelligent commentator from Tocqueville forward has remarked, is a political animal. When he is not engaged in active agitation, it is fair to presume that something ails him.

Consider the partisans of hope, once called liberals but now identified by several titles, most of them incomprehensible. Once they dreamed of the government as the primary agent of wonderful reforms—as the corrector of corporate excesses and the initiator of noble reforms. Many would go to bed on Christmas Eve and dream of Franklin

Roosevelt. Some would think romantic thoughts about the budgets of John F. Kennedy. Their great moment arrived in the middle of the sixties, when the nation was prosperous and everything seemed possible. Various reforms were instituted. Some worked better than others, but ultimately the partisans of hope were disillusioned by the failure to achieve paradise, as is always the case. With visions of justice dancing in their heads, they were rewarded with little more than modified disorder. They had to satisfy themselves with little more than the unhappy acknowledgement that the world was complicated, and that some of its problems are virtually insoluble. Some have continued to promote the government as the agent of virtue in the affairs of the Republic, but with less conviction than before. Most have simply sat back, and puffed their pipes, and wondered what the hell it all means.

If the bugaboo has been kept alive through the late 1970s, it has been done mainly by the people who call themselves conservatives. Their chief bugaboos have been abortions, unbalanced budgets, and taxes. But the history of their crusades has hardly been one to encourage bugaboo watchers. The abortion controversy assumes the aspect of an interminable yowling and yapping, in which the hotheads simply do not have the votes to carry their argument and so might as well close down their tents and await the invasion of some new fever in their camp. The issue of budgets promises little more than a temporary outlet for some fundamentalist rhetoric; it may have staying power, but not as an inflammatory issue. And what can be said of taxes that has not been said before? To be sure, Howard Jarvis, aided by the forces of a bugaboo-starved press, worked admirable magic in making this a hot item for a few months in 1978. There were widespread rumors that the citizens of the Republic were rising up to hang their tax collectors. The howling Jarvis had everyone from the postman to the Speaker of the U. S. House of Representatives saluting him and praising his name. Concerned citizens announced that until taxes were lowered, serenity could not possibly return to this Eden of ours. But, before too long, people started to recognize the institutional havoc that might result if Jarvis were permitted to continue playing Jahweh to America: the police would be laid off, the garbage would go uncollected, the schools would close. A subsequent election brought in mixed returns, the various parties dispersed, and the Jarvis show was closed down by a resurgent case of civic responsibility.

The greatest restraint on bugaboos has been the increased willingness of Americans to believe that their problems are complex, and even international in origin. Grimfaced politicians have been preaching this sermon for some time now, but there has been great reluctance to accept it. Far more powerful was the conviction that Americans are masters of their own destinies, and also of anyone else's if they should choose to interfere. Vietnam was the rudest interruption of this dream, but there have also been others. Consider the "energy crisis." At first it seemed that Exxon, Phillips, Shell, Atlantic Richfield and the rest of the great oil firms were about to be made the subject of a great bugaboo hunt. The foam began to form in the mouths of the usual people, and corporate representatives began appearing on television to drone their defenses of capitalism. But the excitement lasted barely a season. It became clear that a chronic condition had developed, less drastic than at its inception but still unpleasant enough to try men's souls. At the same time it was almost impossible to moralize about this issue, and the bugaboo hunter is invariably dependent on his talent for moralization. At best, he could go home and sulk at the sheiks of Araby. Similar feelings have controlled the national response to various crises, wars and revolutions abroad in the years since the United States ceased bombing Vietnam. Once it was possible for a senator to speak of America's having "lost" China and not get laughed at. Today, with the exception of an occasional wandering general or State Department official, there is no one who assumes that other countries are ours to lose. Together with the experience of various inept bureaucracies at home, this has induced the quiescent frustration which now seems to prevail. There is as much tolerance of the vicissitudes of public life as of the mutations of private life, but this is a long way from hearty acceptance and approval.

Perhaps I am wrong, and, even as I write, some ferocious inflammation is about to rock the land. Certainly in the past year the ladies and gentlemen of the left have displayed remarkable resilience in advancing nuclear energy toward full status as a national bugaboo. With the able assistance of one incident and one movie, they may now be able to live in their accustomed style by alarming the public for several years to come. There is at least a nice symmetry to their indignant outbursts, as they offer solar energy in opposition to the nasty nukes with all the innocent enthusiasm of temperance ladies forecasting heaven on earth after the elimination of demon rum.

In any case the moods will change, as they always do. But at the moment the 1980s promise to be no more interesting than the 1970s, a decade which featured the sort of puzzling but uninspired movement which can be seen in the shifting of sand.

IV. AGONIZERS, GROUCHES AND BORES

Consider the state of the political arts in America. Once the engines of powerful quarrels, the political parties

have been reduced to mere instruments of individual convenience. A lowly congressional candidate can with im-
punity run for office by denouncing an incumbent president
of his own party. Everyone else simply runs against Washington. Even Presidents do it. The Republicans have in
their half-witted fashion moved toward identifying themselves as the party of common conservatism, rather than as
the party of money they used to be, while the Democrats
are the party of everything else. This makes them more the
party of simple expedience. They tend to be faster on their
feet, and they compose a large majority.

There remain many dreary personalities and insub-
stantial ideas. With the recent ascent to bliss eternal of
Messrs. Humphrey and Rockefeller, there are fewer distinctive figures on the political scene than at any time in recent
memory. There is hardly even a real rabble-rouser to be
found, let alone anyone at the top or near it who shows any
symptoms of excellence in the art of governing men. The
President of the United States, his cabinet, the members of
the Senate and the members of the House of Representatives add up to 550 dull oddities. What is it possible to
make of such a man as Carter? Here is someone who organizes and executes a campaign for the presidency as fabulous as any in the history of these United States. Yet he
proves, upon taking office, that he is one of the least interesting men in creation. The man is no more impressive
than a grocery clerk. He is no more intelligent than a trade
union vice president. He is no more handsome than a professor of library science. He is no more eloquent than a bus
driver. He is no more skillful at the management of men
than a summer camp counselor. And yet he was elected
President after having exposed himself more broadly to
public view than any man in the nation's history.

He managed it through his doggedness and his skill at posing—that is to say, by cultivating the same qualities as young women aspiring to become prized models at *Vogue* magazine. Such is the art of politics these days that its master is a mere interpreter of public opinion polls who is able to affect a satisfactory posture after completing his interpretation. Even more representative of the breed than Carter is the preposterous governor of California, the erstwhile seminarian and would-be President, "Jerry" Brown. Here is a fellow who roars against Proposition X one day, grimly witnesses the defeat of this proposition by the voters the following day, sleeps and meditates on his hard floor the third day, and rises on the fourth to proclaim the wisdom of the people in passing the proposition. Having mastered this gimmick, he hauls it out again and again, and furthermore harangues the press on the high virtue of its employment. He flies off to the distant state of New Hampshire to perform as an evangelical cutter of taxes, presuming that this will score some points in advance of the state's presidential primary. He arrives and discovers that his appearance is offensive to the members of his own party inside the state. Does he then behave as an honorable man would, by delivering his speech and then employing his best persuasive powers in assuaging the dissidents within his party? Of course not: he snubs his hosts, serves up a sermon on the high virtue of not offending fellow Democrats, and then hops aboard the next plane back to California. Then, just as he worries that his image might be getting a bit tedious, he at last allows public evidence that he is romantically involved with a famous rock singer and departs with her on a tour of African states. It does not much matter what he says or does as long as he continues to look interesting to a jaded populace. He is a shameless zany, and yet he might reach the top: it is largely a question of whether the American people generally are as stupid as the people of California.

The only politicians who need not read the polls before affecting their postures are those who have captured a consistent constituency, and so may thump as the champions of principle, like the hilarious Ronald Reagan; or those who can appeal directly to man's superstitious and sentimental instincts, like Edward Kennedy. Most of the posturing of recent years has been done in one of two poses —that of agony or that of grouchiness. When the Vietnam war was flaming, the division was fairly interesting. Those in favor of prosecuting the war freely denounced the lily-livered sentimentalists and bums who were opposed, thus enticing the support of the sour-stomached section of the citizenry. Those in opposition to the war were highly adept at recognizing the "anguish of America" and prophesying doom if the young, the poor and the black were not treated with sufficient sensitivity. More recently there has been a distinct swing toward grouchiness among American politicians. The deacon Carter, after all, first campaigned for President by promising a government as full of love as the American people, and thus placed himself in the party of those trying to relieve America's agony. More recently he has joined the Jacobinical advocates of austerity and has tried to appear tough. The fact that he has done this with budgets exceeding half a trillion dollars is quite beside the point: the image is the thing.

All this preening before the cameras makes it difficult for politicians to sustain public interest in themselves, especially after they have reached the top. Swami Brown can send up another smoke screen and yell for constitutional conventions to resolve the dilemmas of the Republic, but he must hatch a new scheme every month or the voters will wonder if he is losing his touch. Having written his rules for the game, he must continue to play by them. A President of the United States is a perpetual prisoner of circumstance. So the prospects for Carter's canonization now appear dim. Whether he appears to be performing competently or in an atmosphere of tortured frustration, his image remains dull. It will require the most ardent revisionist to elevate him to the level of James Knox Polk on the roster of beloved Presidents. His sleepy evangelism has not helped him, surely, but he is bothered even more by the increasingly common suspicion that political leaders are incapable of really great deeds, and that the power of the United States in the world is fading. Public fascination with the leaders who embodied that power fades with it. Even such professional hero-worshipers as Theodore H. White and Arthur Schlesinger, Jr., display symptoms of the malaise. White composes memoirs in which he wonders why he so often trusted the word of magnificoes, while Schlesinger writes academic obituaries for the imperial presidency and churns out another vast monument to Camelot in which the passionate precision of his best work is absent.

The American people are by no means inspired to believe that there are wiser and more capable men waiting in the wings. If they turn to another in the next election, it will be done as much out of boredom as out of conviction. I discern no great popular uprising on behalf of the Swami, the Gipper or King Arthur III. I doubt the advertised yearnings for His Holiness, John Connolly, to lead crusades on behalf of the dollar he devalued in days of yore. I do not expect Lord Ford to be summoned from the eighteenth hole to pacify the world's belligerents with a few rounds of dry martinis in the clubhouse. But anything can happen, and nothing will be too surprising. Americans these days have too much evidence of plain ineffectuality to suppose that their leaders are either heroes or hobgoblins. They simply grow tired of them more quickly, and scout the landscape for new sources of amusement. I doubt that this is a sign that the Republic has achieved a kind of political maturity. Americans in the past seemed happy to believe that their leaders were great men, whether they came in the mold of the booming Roosevelts or the placid Eisenhower. Their skepticism these days is far from serene, and poor Carter appears as much a victim as a progenitor of the national confusion.

In place of ideas there are only moods. I, like most Americans, cast my ballot according to such moods, which are inspired by the transient images on the television screen, and in the papers and newsmagazines. Once I have ascertained that two candidates for office are figures of comparable dishonesty, I push the lever. If I am inclined to regard my fellow Americans with contempt I will vote one way; if I feel pity toward them I will vote another way. But I almost always vote, for the same reason I almost always brush my teeth at night: to satisfy my own hygienic yearnings, and to pacify those who worry about me.

Farewell

These meditations are at an end. I have surveyed enough of the scene for now, and, as a matter of courtesy, I would like to leave a few areas of the world open for the Reichs and Tofflers to explore. I would not dream of robbing them of their caviar. And so I rock back, relight my cigar, and contemplate my cognac. I attempt to think great thoughts about America, in the manner popularized by Mr. Eric Sevareid, but I find after a few moments that my head hurts, and so I give up the game. What can I say? I am sufficiently tickled and provoked by my life here to keep me amused and alert. I am grateful enough, and would recite a pledge of allegiance to the flag if any of my old schoolteachers were to arrive and demand it of me. But let us not get carried away.